Profile
of the
Perfect Person

PROFILE OF THE PERFECT PERSON

Based on The Bhagavad Gītā Chapter II

JAYA ROW

JAICO PUBLISHING HOUSE

Mumbai • Delhi • Bangalore • Kolkata
Hyderabad • Chennai • Ahmedabad • Bhopal

Published by Jaico Publishing House
121 Mahatma Gandhi Road
Mumbai - 400 001
jaicopub@vsnl.com
www.jaicobooks.com

PROFILE OF THE PERFECT PERSON
ISBN 81-7992-126-3

First Jaico Impression: 2004
Fourth Jaico Impression: 2006

Printed by
Snehesh Printers
320-A, Shah & Nahar Ind. Est. A-1
Lower Parel, Mumbai - 400 013.

Dedicated to the Guru

Acknowledgements:
Sirsha Chatterjee for her editorial assistance

NOTE ON TRANSLITERATION AND PRONUNCIATION

In the book, Sanskrit words are transliterated into Roman script according to the scheme adopted by the International Congress of Orientalists at Athens in 1912. Since then, it is generally acknowledged and accepted universally. This scheme is as follows:-

अ	a		son
आ	ā		master
इ	i		if
ई	ī		feel
उ	u		put
ऊ	ū		pool
ऋ	ṛ	*	rhythm
ए	e		play
ऐ	ai		my
ओ	o		oh
औ	au		loud
.	ṁ		Anusvāra (nasalisation of preceding vowel) written like the dot above अ in अंश:
:	ḥ		Visarga (aspiration of preceding vowel) written like the two dots after अंश:

क	k		skate	
ख	kh	*	blockhead	
ग	g		gate	
घ	gh	*	loghut	
ङ	ṅ		sing	
च	c		chuckle	
छ	ch	*	catch him	
ज	j		john	
झ	jh	*	hedgehog	
ञ	ñ	*	bunch	
ट	ṭ	*	start	tongue on upper palate
ठ	ṭh	*	anthill	tongue on upper palate
ड	ḍ	*	dart	tongue on upper palate
ढ	ḍh	*	godhead	tongue on upper palate
ण	ṇ	*	under	tongue on upper palate
त	t	*	French 't'	tongue on upper teeth
थ	th	*	therapy	tongue on upper teeth
द	d	*	then	tongue on upper teeth
ध	dh	*	breathe here	tongue on upper teeth
न	n		numb	tongue on upper teeth
प	p		spin	
फ	ph	*	loophole	
ब	b		bin	
भ	bh	*	abhor	
म	m		much	
य	y		young	
र	r		drama	
ल	l		luck	
व	v		avert	
श	ś	*	show	
ष	ṣ	*	bushell	
स	s		so	
ह	h		hum	

* There are no exact equivalents for the letters listed with asterisks

What is the Bhagavad Gītā?

WHAT IS THE BHAGAVAD GĪTĀ?

The Bhagavad Gītā, or 'Celestial Song', is part of the larger epic, the Mahābhārata, composed by the sage Vyāsa, the first guru to codify the Vedas, the source of all knowledge. Consisting of 701 verses compiled into 18 chapters, the Gītā is Lord Kṛṣṇa's advice to Arjuna on the science of life.

THE NEGATIVE V/S THE POSITIVE

The backdrop of the Gītā is the rivalry between two sets of cousins, the five virtuous Pāṇḍavas and the hundred bad and vicious Kauravas. Duryodhana, the eldest Kaurava prince, deceitfully usurps the kingdom from the Pāṇḍavas. The battle lines are drawn when even Kṛṣṇa's attempts at reconciliation fail with the adamant Duryodhana.

Arjuna and Duryodhana, commanders-in-chief of their respective armies, seek Kṛṣṇa's help. Kṛṣṇa offers his armies to one and himself, alone and unarmed, to the other. Arjuna wisely chooses Kṛṣṇa, while Duryodhana is more than happy to take the armies. It is Kṛṣṇa's valuable advice that finally tilts the balance in the Pāṇḍavas' favour.

The Pāṇḍavas and Kauravas represent the good and evil

within each individual. The evil forces are always larger in number, the good ones are fewer. Both attempt to gain control of the personality. In this conflict, if the positive qualities submit to the higher, the highest being Kṛṣṇa or *Ātman* within us, they can defeat the negative forces and emerge victorious.

THE SYMBOLIC BATTLEFIELD OF LIFE

The Bhagavad Gītā is an external dramatisation of an internal phenomenon. The world is full of challenges, represented by the battlefield in which Arjuna, the individual, is placed. Overwhelmed by the challenge before him, Arjuna breaks down, paralysed, unable to act. He refuses to fight. Ironically it is Arjuna who is the most competent among the Pāṇḍavas, best trained, fully prepared for battle.

When the two armies assemble on the field, all in battle mode, Arjuna asks Kṛṣṇa, his charioteer, to drive him between the armies for a last minute reconnaissance. He sees his beloved ancestor Bhīṣma, his own revered guru Droṇācārya, and a host of his own family members and friends. All aligned with the opposing army. Emotions cloud his judgement. His resolve to fight the battle is shaken and the mighty Arjuna falls! He is unable to act.

VICTORY OVER CHALLENGES

Many of us find ourselves in this predicament. The student all set for the examination collapses with last minute nerves, the job aspirant with dream qualifications fails in the interview because of anxiety, the housewife eager to impress guests messes up her cooking, or a CEO, otherwise an expert negotiator, bungles at the crucial moment... Faced with the inevitable challenges before us, we flounder and fail. The Bhagavad Gītā reconstructs our personality. And empowers us with the technique of living. With this knowledge Arjuna was able to lift himself and gain victory. And so will you.

Introduction

INVEST - INDIA!

For centuries India has been the spiritual leader of the world. Even today, this land of the divine beckons the world to its shores to seek out the greater truths of life and beyond. Scores of institutions and organisations impart spiritual knowledge to seekers in search of peace.

Yet modern India features nowhere among the stalwarts of the world. There seems to be a vacuum in values, work culture and ethics. Norms of life have changed to accommodate petty vested interests. Why? Has the timeless formula of the Bhagavad Gītā lost its relevance in contemporary life? Or are we not applying the formula properly? The answer is, sadly, the latter.

This formula is nothing but a scientific set of rules; eternal laws that are infallible. When properly applied, it cannot but work. We are unable to reap the benefits of this science simply because we have not applied it. We respect the Bhagavad Gītā, but the treasure promised in its verses is not being tapped. Mere worship with no application is as ridiculous as keeping a physics book in the *pūjā* room and worshipping it. But not reading it!! A colossal waste of time and effort in today's fast-paced world, wouldn't you say? Science in the laboratory is of little use unless converted to technology in our homes.

There is a dire need for technology transfer from the Bhagavad Gītā into our lives. This is not taking place because there is an erroneous belief that the philosophy is out of sync with modern times. That one needs to retire to the Himālayas to apply it. But just for one moment take a look at the context of the Bhagavad Gītā, a sermon delivered in the middle of a battlefield!! What greater proximity to real-life situations can there be? Arjuna, the talented, courageous, highly-skilled warrior, referred to as *savyasāci* (ambidextrous) as symbolic of his exceptional abilities, breaks down while he faces the greatest battle of his life. And is unable to use any of his multi-faceted resources. He falls to the depths of depression and is incapacitated. Kṛṣṇa props up his spirit with timeless wisdom, reaches into the recesses of his mind and restores his inner balance with righteous belief and clear thinking. He convinces him to fight with vigour, courage and valour. Significantly Arjuna wakes up to his calling, fights and wins.

WHY THE BHAGAVAD GĪTĀ?

We are all well trained in our respective fields of expertise. But faced with challenging circumstances we crumble and all the knowledge we have so painstakingly acquired lies in utter disuse. So alongside academic qualifications and cutting edge technology, we need to empower ourselves from within to face challenges and emerge victorious. The world today is like an enormous ocean with daunting waves. If we wait for the waves to subside we will be waiting forever. Instead if we learn to surf them, the experience becomes enjoyable. In fact the more formidable the waves, the greater the thrill! We need to master the technique of riding over the challenges the world throws at us instead of buckling under pressure.

This is what the Bhagavad Gītā gives us: the power to face the challenges and emerge victorious. The greater the challenges of this roller coaster ride through life, the more proficient we become and the greater we enjoy the swings.

THE SALT OF LIFE

We assume that the philosophy of the Bhagavad Gītā is meant to provide solace for the aged and those retired from active life. Yet it is the most important ingredient in our lives today, the salt of life. Trying to live life without the Gītā is like eating food without salt. In the cuisine of any country, the most delectable dishes are tasteless without salt. Yet just a dash of salt can make even a simple meal delicious. The Bhagavad Gītā provides us with this salt in our lives.

Why are we so bored with everything around us? It is because this essential ingredient is missing from our lives.

We think that enjoyment lies in the external world and we do everything to entertain ourselves with the enticing world. How futile are our efforts! The enjoyment comes, only to leave us with a feeling of emptiness before we set out for the next attraction. The Bhagavad Gītā tells us that true enjoyment, the real salt in life, lies inside us and nothing external can make this dish of life tastier. Once we discover this magic within us, the world remaining the same, all enjoyment will be ours.

SUCCESS THROUGH INNER UNFOLDING

All over the world people clamour for success, excellence. They want prosperity but they experience stumbling blocks, impediments, and reverses. Work becomes strenuous. It is like driving a car with one foot on the accelerator and the other on the brake! The Bhagavad Gītā removes the retarding forces, helps us gain mastery over ourselves and conquer the world. Juxtaposing the Gītā with our daily life opens the doors to success. For this we need to know what we are made of.

Our personality is composed of the following entities:

- **The body** is our outer layer which receives stimuli from the world and responds to them by way of actions.

- **The mind** is the home of emotions and feelings. It generates loves and hates, creates whims and fancies and functions on impulse.

- **The intellect** is that which differentiates between pairs of opposites. It is the abode of rationality, analysis, judgement.

- **The Spirit** — referred to as *Ātman* — is your real Self. It breathes life into the lifeless body, mind and intellect.

WHO AM I?

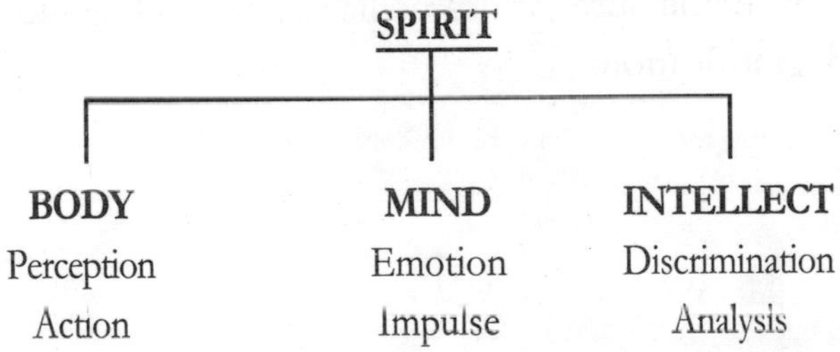

Living beings that we are, act we must at each moment. This action can be driven by the mere impulse of the mind or be guided by the sane counsel of the intellect. Often the two lead to divergent paths. Which one should we follow? The will-o'-the-wisp of the mind or the clear decision of the intellect?

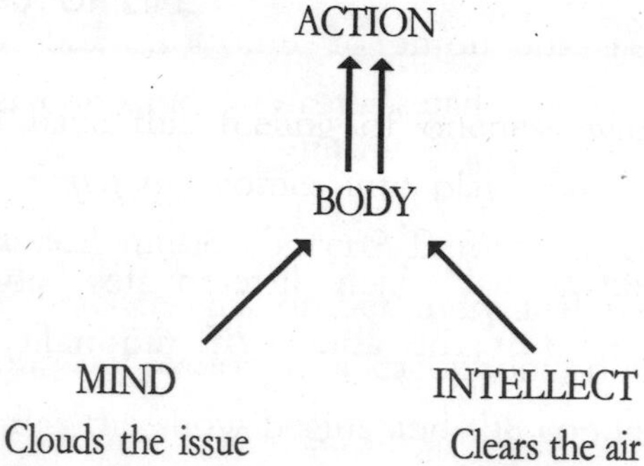

To determine this we need to understand the mind and intellect better. The mind is just a flow of thoughts that grabs at instant joys. It is incapable of discerning what is in our long-term interest and what is not. It is the intellect that can set aside the lure of immediate joys and guide us to deferred gratification.

PASSWORD TO SUCCESS

The mind can be likened to a virus in a computer; the intellect is like anti-virus software. The virus corrupts the data. The anti-virus software protects it from present and future viruses. Similarly the mind renders all previously acquired knowledge useless. Only the intellect is able to access that knowledge and apply it. Today we are all trying to add greater knowledge, skill and expertise to our matrix for success. But no one pays attention to how much of the acquired knowledge is actually applied at the workplace. When you need the skill the most, it eludes you.

A student goes well prepared for his exam but in the exam hall he is overwhelmed by anxiety – 'Will I pass or not?' The mind plays up, the knowledge deserts him and he cannot answer the simplest of questions.

A housewife is an expert cook. But when there are guests for dinner she works herself into a frenzy. She puts more salt in one dish, overcooks another, burns the third, etc.

In both these instances it is not the lack of knowledge that has caused failure but the inability to access it. Only as long as the intellect is in command of your personality is the knowledge available to you. When the mind starts playing up with anxiety, tension and nervousness, you are unable to do the simplest of things! What is the use of the scrupulously gained knowledge if you cannot use it when you need it the most? And what is it that denies it to you? **Your own mind.**

So what is the password to success? **The intellect.** This is the basic premise of Vedānta, its very crux. Many centuries ago, in the golden era, every child in India was taught this paramount knowledge along with other skills. And as he grew to adulthood in full control of his mind, the tricky situations of life were well within his grasp. Today this knowledge, the most essential ingredient of success, is lost even in India.

Thus the world is in turmoil. People today have a great deal more knowledge than they did in the past. But there is a huge gap between knowledge and application. It is this lacuna that Vedānta addresses. Educational institutions, corporate bodies and governments need to bridge this gap. Instead they only give additional information, burdening the individual further. True education is development of your mind and intellect so that they work **for** you and not **against** you.

WORK — DRUDGERY OR REVELRY?

What is your attitude towards work? One of boredom and burdensome obligation. Leading to stress and dullness. You may believe that if you change your office address from the distant suburbs to an upmarket metropolitan area you will find enthusiasm for work. All that happens is that the expenditure increases. And the initial excitement evaporates!

So what is it that makes work exciting? It is not the job *per se* but the attitude towards it. For example, the same chore of changing diapers can be revelry for the mother but drudgery for the babysitter.

What are you working for? Is it only for a personal trophy, for remuneration? Or are you dedicating your work to a higher cause beyond yourself? Develop the right attitude towards your job and even the most mundane work becomes a source of joy. Then your **vocation** becomes a **vacation**.

Svāmī Rāma Tīrtha, when invited to lecture in America, titled his speech, 'Make Every Night a Christmas Night and Every Day a New Year's Day'. What a wonderful way to spend the year! If we could make every day an occasion to celebrate, our whole life becomes one long party! That is what happens when you have a higher ideal. Otherwise you may change your location, have the plushest office in Manhattan, but you will be as bored as you are now. So this is the trick the Bhagavad Gītā teaches us. Kindle your soul with the spirit of a higher ideal, douse the fire of hatred and bitterness with the power of love and light the flame of wisdom which empowers you and there is nothing in the world you will not achieve.

ENJOY SUCCESS

Not many people become successful. The few who have achieved success find they are unable to enjoy it. As the Bhagavad Gītā says, 'they cook but eat sin'. They work hard but all they get in return is mental torment, sin. A person who has the means cannot enjoy while the person who has the appetite to enjoy does not have the resources. Once an object of desire becomes available, a person goes all out and indulges in it. Every contact only fans the fire of a new desire. None satisfies fully and all perish with time. Experiences that thrill on the first encounter pall at the fiftieth. Economists call it the 'Law of Diminishing Returns'.

So this is how you go about losing your enjoyment. By the time you are an adult everything becomes insipid. Nothing thrills you. The Bhagavad Gītā gives you that unique formula to enjoy life such that you retain the novelty of every experience till the end of life. How foolishly you deprive yourself of this rich formula. You think that it takes away enjoyment when in fact it gives back the enjoyment you have lost by reckless indulgence in sense objects.

MEANINGFUL RELATIONSHIPS

You go out in search of relationships. Yet you feel isolated even in the company of dear ones. The truth is that you are isolated from your inner being and the higher Force that governs you. Thus you are disharmonious with the whole. To restore that connection, you try and form bonds in the hope of finding peace, enjoyment and that elusive sense of completeness. But alas, desire and ego throttle interpersonal communication. You then convince yourself that the problem lies with the other person. In your endeavour to change the other person you only make things worse. You make a living hell for yourself.

The Bhagavad Gītā shows us how to enjoy relationships and not make them into accidents of life. It teaches us to replace clashes and collisions with courtesy and co-operation. All we need to do is turn the situation around, look at things from the other person's perspective. Put yourself in the other's shoes. You will find that the love, understanding and courtesy is returned, making the interaction a wonderful experience. You might say: 'How can I have love and affection for my mother-in-law? You do not know how terrible and nasty she is!' Yet in your own experience when you have come across a similar situation you have overcome it. Let us see how.

How does a mother react when her little son returns from school? He had left for school in white, immaculate clothes. But when he comes back how does he look? Black and dirty with mud in his hair and ink all over his shirt. He comes back sweaty, smelly, dirty. But the mother doesn't say, "O God, you're so dirty!" She welcomes him with a hug. Not only that, the fact that he is covered with mud is, in itself, a source of joy for her. Apply the same formula to the mother-in-law. Try it, it works!

The truth is that each one of us is a combination of beauty and ugliness within. One may have a foul temper, another is wicked, a third selfish. Something or the other is wrong with all of us. The question comes down to **focus.** If you focus on the dirt, of course it will repel you. You will hate the person. But if you have the ability to laser through the dirt and zero in on the fine person behind it all then you will get the same thrill as the mother gets when she sees her son covered with dirt. What a wonderful experience! Then you will be in a state of constant jubilation and cheer. Instead today every person you come across irritates you. Once you learn to focus on the good in a person while glossing over the bad, the faults become a source of amusement to you!

This is the art that the Bhagavad Gītā teaches us, enriching us at every contact with the external world. This is what all spiritually enlightened persons achieve. They are unable to see evil in anybody. Learn to focus on the beauty in everyone. Connect with them at that level, bringing out hidden talents and the best in them and you will convert a motley group of average players into an all-star team! Today because the focus is on faults you reduce a team of stars to a mediocre squad.

INSIGHTS THAT EMPOWER

Just as there are laws governing the external world, like the law of gravity, there are laws governing your inner world. They apply universally with no exceptions. Ignorance of the laws does not exempt you from their effects. So you would do well to learn these laws and abide by them in order to have a pleasant sojourn through life. If you don't learn these laws you will be like the early airmen. Many years ago, before the laws of aerodynamics were known, the human being watched birds flying and desired to emulate their flight. He designed a crude contraption that resembled a bird, took it to the top of a cliff and jumped off. The machine was actually an unsupported object hurtling towards the earth at an alarming speed. But for a few tantalising moments he believed he was in flight. He was not in flight as he was not in compliance with the laws of aerodynamics. He was in free fall.

Similarly you and I live life without learning its laws. When you violate a law what happens? Temporarily you may feel good. When you cut corners, compromise on values, you feel you've beaten the system. The truth is you are not in flight, you are in free fall. It is just that the consequences of your actions are far removed in time and space and you have lulled yourself into complacence. But sooner or later the law catches up with everybody.

Then you compound the problem by attributing your setbacks to the world and try to correct it! All you have to do is learn the basic laws of life and living. Once you learn these laws, comply with them, abide by them, you will find life becoming easy.

THE RIGHT CHOICE

Only the human being has the unique gift of choosing his or her actions. Vegetarian or non-vegetarian, aggrandising or sacrificial, noble or bestial. Therefore it is imperative to know what to choose. The intellect helps to make the right choice. Develop it, strengthen it. Today the intellect is totally neglected. And you are full of wrong concepts. This is the root cause of all your problems. So dedicate yourself to educate yourself.

TAP YOUR POTENTIAL

The Bhagavad Gītā shows you how to tap your real potential. Only the human being can grow to a divine being. As Shakespeare said in 'Hamlet', "What a piece of work is a man! How noble in reason! How infinite in faculty, in apprehension how like a god!" Science says that we use between 1 to 10% of our potential and the balance 90-99% of what we are worth remains unknown. Most of us live and die without so much as a glimpse of who we are and what we bring into this world. What a tragedy! So what is this potential and how do you grow up to it?

What happens from the time you are born till you become a full-grown adult? An infant is never content to lie on its back. It uses all its might to turn over, opening up a whole new world. But it doesn't stop with that. It struggles to move forward, to crawl, to sit up, to stand, to walk. And so it goes on right till it becomes an adult. But once it becomes an adult the goal seems to be to somehow maintain status quo!

Now what the Bhagavad Gītā tells you is that as a full-grown adult, you are still a spiritual infant. You need to move from spiritual infancy to spiritual adolescence. And then to real adulthood. That unfortunately is not automatic. You have to put in a lot of effort for this metamorphosis to take place. But if you resist that growth, you will be like the caterpillar regretting that someday it will have to leave the leaf it is nibbling on to soar aloft. It worries that one day it will have to take to the skies and bask in the sun. Imagine the difference between the caterpillar's life and the butterfly's life! The gap between you and spiritual adulthood is even greater than that!

VISION

So have that vision. Vision is the ability to see the invisible. Visualise and start moving. Grow… from the level of mere physical delights right up to the spiritual.

SPIRIT

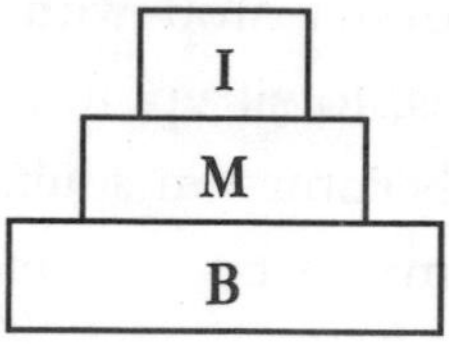

EMOTIONAL MOTIVATION

When you move from the physical to the emotional level you find a whole new source of energy. You are able to transcend the limitation of your physical body and work in a different realm altogether.

For instance when Sachin Tendulkar played in the World Cup in 1999 against Kenya soon after his father's death, he suffered from jet lag, physical exhaustion and the grief of having lost his father. But he scored a magnificent 140 runs which he dedicated to his father. Where did he get the energy from? From the fact that he was inspired. This is emotional motivation, which gave him that burst of energy.

Ian Thorpe, nicknamed "Thorpedo" because of his amazing seven gold medals in the Sydney Olympics, is another example. By his own admission he had reached a stalemate in his career. And then a dear friend of his, a younger boy, was diagnosed with cancer. That got him to think about what he was doing. His attitude changed. His friend could not afford the treatment that was necessary. So he pledged his income and endorsements to his friend and to all the other children who were in the same predicament. And he says it was this that gave him the tremendous urge to put in a fantastic performance. This is the power of emotional motivation.

INTELLECTUAL DRIVE

If you move even higher and you are driven by an intellectual ideal you have access to far greater reserves of energy and vitality than you ever imagined. An example of this is Gandhījī and the Independence movement. Here was a group of people with no resources at their command. They did not have financial backing or political clout. They had nothing except the intellectual ideal. And that was enough for them to achieve independence from the then mighty British Empire.

THE POWER OF THE SPIRIT

Move still further and you ascend to the spiritual goal. If you are able to act and make every action of yours an offering of worship towards that divine Force – the Force that has bestowed you with that ability in the first place – then there is nothing you cannot achieve. Poetically put in a Sanskrit verse, the power of the Spirit is such that it 'makes a mute speak, makes a lame person climb mountains'. In other words we gain infinite power.

And what must you do? Chapter IX of the Bhagavad Gītā has the most exquisite verse to describe this attitude of dedication. To the highest Power offer '*patram, puṣpam, phalam, toyam*' a leaf, a flower, a fruit. And if you cannot even manage that, offer water. But give it with a feeling of dedication.

George Herbert expresses the same thought in 'The Elixir'.

'A servant with this clause
Makes drudgery divine,
Who sweeps a room as for thy law,
Makes that and the action fine'.

A UNIQUE ANALOGY

The TV game show, 'Kaun Banega Crorepati?', the Indian version of 'Who Wants to be a Millionaire?' is a great analogy of life and spirituality. The game gives four options – three wrong, one right. In life, too, we have four avenues to choose from – body, mind, intellect and *Ātman*. Body, mind and intellect are the wrong choices, *Ātman* is the correct one. If we always choose *Ātman*, we will be not just 'Crorepatis', but 'Infinitepatis'!

KAUN BANEGA INFINITEPATI?

BODY	**MIND**
INTELLECT	*ĀTMAN*

As in the game show, we have three lifelines. The first is the conscience that discerns between right and wrong. You need to listen to the conscience. As someone said, "All the world needs is an amplifier for that still, small voice." But if you don't listen to your conscience, you get Viṣṇu's *gada* or a knock on the head. You fall on hard times, suffer losses, face difficulties. This helps you to think. But if even that doesn't make you think about the consequences of your actions, then you get not a 'lifeline' but a 'deathline'—the *cakra*. You will be destroyed by your own actions.

And the reward, the prize, is Infinite. The entire gist of the philosophy in one simple game show. So now get ready to be in the 'hot seat'!

AS YOU THINK SO YOU BECOME

Schopenhauer said, "I am who I want to be." The law of life tells us that as we think so we become. So the trick is to constantly think about what you want to become.

A young boy went home in tears and told his mother he was not selected in the team because he was too small. The mother said, "It is not the size of the person in the game that matters but the size of the game in the person". He understood. The next morning he woke up early and started practising. He practised relentlessly. When the next season came he tried again and made it to the team. And thus he went on. His name? Michael Jordan, the basketball great.

Spiritual life is about persistent thoughts of *Ātman*. Spiritual exercise or worship is not to be done once in a while. Part-time spirituality is of no use as it gets washed away into oblivion by other diverse thoughts. Spirituality is not a casual, passing interest. It is a consistent focus on the Truth. Then what happens to the mundane affairs of life, one may ask. How does one conduct one's affairs in the world if one is immersed in spiritual thoughts all the while?

SINGLE FOCUS, MULTIPLE TASKS

The Bhagavad Gītā shows a unique way out. You are capable of multi-tasking or concentrating on more than one job at a time. While driving you adjust the rear-view mirror, speak on the cellphone, change the music and yet do not take your attention off the road even for a second.

An efficient housewife manages cooking, cleaning, supervising the maid and catching up on neighbourhood gossip simultaneously, while her attention is focused on the baby!

Similarly in the journey of life towards Self Realisation, you perform innumerable mundane tasks, perceive the world, act, feel emotions, judge with the intellect. But if you ever take your attention off *Ātman*, there will be 'accidents'. You will be riddled with confusion, problems and trauma.

THE REAL CHALLENGE

Every one of us goes through some dejection, anger, fear, sadness and agitation. But we attribute it all to the external world. The truth is that the world has no power to posit a challenge to us. The real challenge lies within us. To maintain our focus on the supreme Truth in and through our daily transactions in the world. To the extent that we are able to maintain this focus, we are spiritual. Spiritual life is not just going on pilgrimages, observing fasts or engaging in hours of rituals. What determines your spiritual status is whether your thoughts are invested in the higher.

CLASSICAL LIVING: OASIS OF PEACE

In Indian classical music, it is important to align one's attention with one note, *sā*. Myriad beautiful compositions, soul-lifting *rāgas*, exquisite renditions stem from that single attunement. Every performer finetunes to that unique note before he begins his concert. And this attunement continues right through the performance. But the untrained listener finds the singular drone a nuisance!

Classical living is attunement to that one divine Power while you go through a wide array of perceptions and actions, a range of emotions and a multitude of thoughts. Spiritual knowledge helps achieve this grandeur of living. All the noise, chaos and confusion are outside. In and through the clamour you are able to withdraw into an oasis of peace within. When you are attuned to that tranquillity within, you do not need an environment that lends peace. As Gandhījī said, it is not difficult to find peace in peaceful circumstances. It needs extraordinary character and integrity to retain the peace in a disturbed environment. If you maintain your balance even when the environment is challenging, then alone are you a human being. For only the human being has the ability to attune to the inner peace within, away from the external din.

ENJOY WITHOUT DESIRING

The Bhagavad Gītā says that the source of all mental agitation is your own mind. The mind is full of innumerable desires vying for attention. And you become a victim of your own desires. Thus the key to happiness is reduction of desires. You find this unpalatable because you equate it with denying yourself objects of desire. But that is not what the Bhagavad Gītā prescribes. Nowhere does it say you have to stop enjoying. It merely tells you to stop hankering, craving, lusting after sense objects and becoming a slave to them. **Enjoy them by all means.**

In fact desire prevents you from obtaining as well as enjoying the world. It clouds the mind and distorts reasoning. With a disturbed mind your thinking becomes flawed and actions faulty. As a result success eludes you. And you become discontented and frustrated. Therefore if you want happiness you have to embark on a programme of desire-management. Reduce the bulk of desires, upgrade their quality and re-route them to the higher. As long as you have desire you are at the mercy of objects of desire. It does not become a human being of such outstanding calibre to beg at the portals of inanimate objects! You can possess them. You can have the whole world at your feet. But never desire it. Christ said, "It is as difficult for a rich man to enter the gates of heaven as it is for a camel to enter the eye of a needle". The question is, rich with what? Desires. Not resources. Misunderstanding this, people gave up the scriptures instead!

Once you reach the state of freedom from desire you become a king. Master. No object can hold sway over you. No person can victimise you. In sharp contrast, today every little thing affects you. Food makes or mars your day. Smokers are at the mercy of cigarettes. The list is endless.

VEDĀNTA OPERATING SYSTEMS

The Bhagavad Gītā extols three pathways to excellence. They are *Karma Yoga* (Path of Action), *Bhakti Yoga* (Path of Devotion) and *Jñāna Yoga* (Path of Knowledge) using the body, mind and intellect respectively.

KARMA YOGA

Karma Yoga deals with desires through action. You act. But the moment you get into activity you get caught in a web of desire. The Bhagavad Gītā says: maintain your freedom. Act in the world without getting imprisoned by the very activity you are engaged in. But you are like a spider that spins a web only to get entangled in it. *Karma Yoga* is the technique of action by which you exhaust existing desires without creating fresh ones.

Svadharma – Your Core Interest

The first step is to identify your own unique calling in life, your *svadharma.* Each of us has some inborn talent. A deeply embedded interest, leaning, gift. Identify that and in that field fix a higher ideal. A goal beyond your selfish interests, one that includes a larger segment of humanity.

To perform *Karma Yoga* you do not have to change the field of activity you are engaged in. You only need to finetune your action. Change your attitude towards it. An architect need not become a social worker to be a *karma yogī*. He just needs to work dedicatedly in the field of architecture for the larger good.

THREE TYPES OF ACTION

There are three types of actions. They are categorised on the basis of motivation i.e. the attitude backing the action, not the action itself. The action being the same, it could fall in any of the three grades.

SELFISH ACTION

The first rung on the ladder of actions is selfish action. It is driven by a selfish desire to cater to your own needs or maybe those of the family. You say, "What's in it for me?" Only if you see a return in some way are you interested. If not, you are indifferent to that action. This way, you are catering to the lowest level of your personality. Denying yourself higher enjoyments by your own volition. Thus you are never happy, always desiring more. Your actions have no potency or power. You do not achieve success. Moreover, you are constantly adding to your burden of desires.

UNSELFISH ACTION

When you shift from this to unselfish activity a whole new world opens up before you. An unselfish action is driven by an unselfish desire. For the 'greater common good' – the organisation, city, nation or humanity. The accent shifts from 'what can I get' to 'how can I contribute'. This unleashes tremendous vitality in your actions. When you work for a higher cause, that lofty ideal keeps the mind from devolving into chaos and bad moods. More often than not you find you are cheerful, full of beans, dynamic, active. When you rally your thoughts around a goal the mind is less likely to drift into negative thoughts. A selfish person on the other hand is always pulling a long face, depressed, has no energy or vitality.

The world is not so destitute as to need anyone's service. There is a power that created the universe. It will take care of it with or without your help. So it is not the world that needs your service. You need to serve. For your sheer sustenance, your existence, you have to work for a higher cause. Kṛṣṇa says emphatically: 'This world is not for the one who does not sacrifice'. If you don't have a lofty ideal you will not gain anything, not even make a living. The ideal is the vitamin that fuels performance.

GIVE TO GAIN

You will say, 'What will happen to me if I start serving'? Take a look at those who have worked for a higher cause. See what happens to those who work for themselves. You will find that the givers are the successful ones while the takers are the losers. Svāmī Rāma Tīrtha said, "The way to gain anything is to lose it".

Set aside your interests temporarily and, as if by magic, your needs get taken care of. Give of yourself. Physics tells us that an object is red in colour only because it absorbs all other colours except red. Amazingly, what it gives it retains. So is it with life. Grab, you lose. Give, you gain. THE WAY TO GAIN IS TO LOSE. That is the immortal secret that the Bhagavad Gītā reveals to you.

A person who is obsessed with money invariably loses it. And he loses that for which he has paid a very heavy price – he may have short-changed several people, sacrificed relationships, etc. In the end he loses even the money. So it is a loss all the way!

A person who overlooks his desires and works for something higher gets everything. Mohandās Karamchand Gandhi moved from 'dandy' to Dāṇḍī – he set his sights on the nation, with the thought that every Indian must have the basic necessities of life and only then will I help myself. What happened to him? He became a world icon.

Learn the art of setting aside your personal interests and work for a higher cause. It may appear fearful at first. But it's a win-win situation all the way. The rewards are enormous.

SACRIFICE TO REJOICE

How do we move from selfish to unselfish mode? The Bhagavad Gītā gives us a simple yet significant analogy to explain the meaning of sacrifice. *Yajña* is an ancient ritual that invokes the fire god through incantations. A fire is invoked in a brick trough and the participants offer *āhuti* – ghee or grain – into the fire. When the offering is made the fire leaps up. This signifies the appeasement of the fire god who blesses you.

When Kṛṣṇa tells Arjuna to perform *yajña* in the battlefield he is certainly not asking him to start a fire! Kṛṣṇa has infused a new meaning, breathed new life into an ancient ritual that is no longer relevant in the modern context. Every generation needs to retain the moving spirit behind the rituals and adapt it to changing environments. Re-vitalise, re-invent, innovate, refresh, instead of trying in vain to continue the external form while ignoring the essence. Today there is an urgent need to bring about this rejuvenation.

The *kuṇḍa* is the field of activity one is engaged in, like the organisation one works for. All the employees offer their particular talent. It could be salesmanship, accountancy, managerial skills etc. When everyone contributes his might towards the welfare of the organisation the profits soar. Then automatically everyone gets a slice of the pie. It has a ripple effect. Everyone benefits. This is what Kṛṣṇa is trying to tell Arjuna and, more importantly, all of us. If we don't contribute to the **whole,** all that will be left is a gaping **hole!** Let us all put in our best, our talent, gift, or ability into the *kuṇḍa* of the nation. When the nation profits, the benefits will automatically cascade down to all of us. Out of ignorance we say, 'To each his own. Let me grab a piece of the cake for myself'. We are all busy grabbing. But what is there to grab? Nothing. So contribute first, only then will you receive. More than you ever conceived!

SELFLESS ACTION

The real potency of action is experienced only when you escalate to selfless action. Action not propelled by desire at all. You make a paradigm shift from desire ridden activity to action driven by duty. A need to repay society for the things you have already received. Acting in a spirit of thanksgiving. Offering your talent to that Power which bestowed you with the ability you possess. In the ultimate sense there is no desire for the world. Because you are gripped by a desire for Realisation. Since Realisation is beyond the world this action is considered to be desireless.

PLAY YOUR ROLE

There is the Spirit that has created the universe. It takes care of every living being – virus, bacterium, earthworm, cockroach. When you consider this it seems arrogant and foolish to believe that we can improve what that Power has created. Yet as long as we live we must act. So how should we act? As one of the many players in the divine orchestra of the world. Everyone has a little role to play. Play it to the best of your ability and the orchestra will take care of itself. That is not what we do. We unnecessarily become self-appointed Managing Directors of the universe! In the end we become damaging directors! And bring about wanton destruction, irreparable damage. If you are a musician play to your best level. If you are a cook, cook. If a manager, manage. That is all.

As Shakespeare said,
'All the world's a stage
And all men and women mere players
They have their exits and their entrances.'

Identify your role. Play it to the best of your ability. Without worrying about the result. Only then will you attain the highest level of activity. Every action becomes an act of worship. To that divine Power. This is selfless action.

COLLATERAL BENEFIT

To the extent you are able to lift yourself up from selfish

through unselfish to selfless activity your actions become more potent, dynamic. You become successful. You gain happiness because happiness lies in serving a larger cause. And desires decrease. The mind is fixed on the higher goal. Since you are thinking of the goal your mind does not stray into selfish desires. These desires are then starved. Any desire that is not fed wanes. The higher gets reinforced, the lower vanishes. You benefit in every way. This is *Karma Yoga.*

So fix a higher goal. Act dynamically. Surrender your mind to the goal. Focus your intellect on it. Pursue it consistently, not allowing your actions to deviate from the set path. Concentrate on every action without meandering into the wasteful avenues of past worry, future anxiety or present frenzy. Success, happiness and spiritual growth will be yours.

Bhakti Yoga

Bhakti Yoga is the deployment of emotions to get to Realisation. The by-products of this are success and happiness. First let us see what is not *Bhakti.* It is not begging for things that you are unwilling to work for. It is not asking God to grant your wishes. Even with ordinary love between two people, the moment there is expectation, it ceases to be love. It becomes business.

In business you give with the tacit understanding that you will get something in return. How can you do business in the name of love, how can you do business in the name of devotion? To ask from God when He has already bestowed so much on you is the height of ingratitude.

To make matters worse, you don't even know what to ask for. Since you don't know, it is prudent not to ask. For example in the poem, 'The Olive Tree' by S. Baring Gould, there are two hermits living in neighbouring caves. Both decide that they want to pray to God, for which they need olive oil to light the lamp. Each plants an olive tree to get the oil. One hermit plants the sapling, and prays 'now for sunshine now for rain.' God grants every petition, but in the end, his plant dies. So he goes to his neighbour because he notices that the neighbour's olive tree is thriving. He asks: "Brother, please tell me what you did. I prayed to God to give my olive tree what I thought it needed. He granted everything, and still my olive tree died. Yours is thriving. What's the secret?" The fellow hermit told him: "I planted the tree, I did what I had to do and left the rest to God because 'He who made knew what it needed better than a man like me'."

He who made the whole universe is taking care of every creature so beautifully, can He not take care of you? Does He need your help to take care of you? Ridiculous! Therefore there is no point in asking.

DEFICIENCY MOTIVATION

The essential point is that you already have everything you need. But it is this deadly mind of yours which creates a shortage where there is abundance. The mind has the uncanny knack of picking on one little thing that you don't have. It torments and tortures you such that everything you have is then rendered irrelevant. You struggle and work hard to acquire things of the world. Having acquired them, you make them irrelevant by shifting your focus to something you don't have!

Thus right through life you are driven by what is known as 'deficiency motivation'. You become a beggar when you are a millionaire. Right now, every one of us has enough and more.

So prayer or worship is not begging for things you don't have. It is an intense awareness of the bounty you have been bestowed with. And a deep feeling of gratitude to that Power. You may not know who has granted you all this, but you certainly know that you have been blessed. Gratitude unlocks the fullness of life. It converts what you have into enough and more, so that you don't feel the need to ask for anything. It lends peace, which converts chaos into order, confusion into clarity, an ordinary meal into a feast!

MAKE EVERY MEAL A FEAST!

Youngsters are always on the lookout for excitement. They tell their mother, "Can't we have something different? The same *dal chawal* (lentil and rice) for dinner everyday is boring." They want Mexican one day, Italian the next and so on. But even that ordinary meal becomes a feast if you look at it differently. Think about the grain of rice – its colour, texture, flavour, taste – everything has been designed to perfection. If one thing had gone astray we would not have been able to eat the rice. The best food technologists in the world have not been able to improve upon even a single food item. When you think of it in this way you go into raptures over the simplest of fare. It is in acknowledgement of this natural splendour that there is the tradition of saying a prayer before meals. While Christians say grace, Hindus repeat a verse from the scriptures and so also in every religion of the world.

So devotion is not just *mūrti pūjā*, worship of an idol, but adoration of the *mūrtis* created by God Himself. That's why Mohammed said, 'Do you love God? Then must you love His creatures'. How can you swear allegiance to an unknown entity called God, when you can't love things and beings around you? So the foremost qualification for devotion is that you must love His creation first, then you get to Him.

If you say, 'I hate everybody around me but I love God', it's meaningless.

Hence *bhakti* is not exclusive loyalty to a particular deity or prophet. Nor is it denouncement or destruction of anybody who doesn't concur with your opinion. Right through history the bitterest battles have been fought to 'uphold' religion. *Bhakti* is an understanding that there is diversity in the world. In fact, it is this diversity that lends charm to things. How unique is each living being. It's a designer's world! Everyone is one of a kind. *Bhakti* is an acceptance of this diversity.

THY WILL, NOT MY WILL

When you love another person, the crucial thing is that you must accept the good along with the bad. If you don't accept the person as he is, it is not love. Similarly, if you don't accept God's diversity, if you want everything in alignment with your thoughts and opinions, then you are rejecting God. *Bhakti* is not an assertion of your will against God's but an alignment with and submission to God's will. As the Lord's prayer says, **'Thy will** be done', not **my will.**

DEVOTION – 'APART' TO 'A PART'

One of the ailments that afflicts humanity today is a feeling of isolation, loneliness, separateness from others. This is brought about by desire and ego, which put you on a collision course with people. As a result you may have everything around you but lack emotional security. And it is this loneliness and isolation that drives people to the edge. The feeling of separation from the totality is created by none other than yourself. Because you consider yourself **'apart'** from everyone else, not **'a part'** of the totality.

How can you understand that you are 'a part' of and not 'apart' from others? By identifying with people, by looking for a common cord that binds you to them. By finding a commonality in the differences. Don't look for people who are identical to you. Then life becomes boring. You should look for people with whom you share a common agenda, irrespective of differences. Abraham Lincoln, when he was elected President of the USA, chose as his Secretary of State and Defence Secretary two people who did not like him. They felt he was not qualified to be President. But he chose them because according to him they were best qualified for the job. He genuinely and sincerely worked with them knowing that they shared a common love for the American people and a deep commitment to the nation. And by the end of his term the two people who had disliked him became his most loyal aides and allies.

CENTRIFUGAL TO CENTRIPETAL

In this we learn a lesson. Even if you feel that you're not popular with people, all you have to do is find that common platform. Then you change from being a centrifugal force, one that repels everything in its vicinity, to a centripetal force – one that attracts all. There is a saying, "Some people spread happiness **wherever** they go, others create happiness **whenever** they go!"

So when you have a common agenda you draw people towards you. You become an irresistible, magnetic force like all men of Realisation. Ramaṇa Maharṣi lived in seclusion yet people from all over the world were attracted to him. When you love people they reciprocate. It helps you to win over others and achieve success.

There is an example of what this benevolent attitude can do. A middle class family in Mumbai once got an inflated telephone bill, which was clearly an error on the part of the company. They went to the office with past bills to present their case. They were ushered into the office of a senior manager who was to use his discretion and decide. It was then that the lady of the house thought to herself that they had received good service from the company for many years. Her attitude changed from being confrontational to cooperative. She explained that the billing was incorrect but that she was willing to pay the amount if the manager insisted because she was grateful for the excellent service received in the past. She would, however, consider it as a donation in appreciation of services rendered and not as payment of the bill. Her response stupefied the manager. He asked for time to think about it and the next day waived the entire amount!

ORCHESTRA OF LIFE

When you have this feeling of oneness with people, the arithmetic of synergy comes into play. Have you been to a western classical music concert? Before the concert begins, each artiste practices his or her individual piece separately. This warming up session is a cacophony, not a symphony. But as soon as the show begins and the conductor raises his baton, sweet melody pours forth. What was noise becomes exquisite music. What is the difference? The earlier isolated effort is replaced by performance in unison. This creates a totally different effect.

Imagine the power of the entire nation, if it rose in unison of thought, word and deed to a higher dimension! This is what communication, identification and the feeling of oneness can create in society. In our country in particular we seem to have lost this. Individually we excel. Collectively we seem to lose focus! That shouldn't really be the case. Indian tradition is to conquer people with love, values and knowledge.

MULTIPLY YOUR JOYS

Identify with your neighbour. His joys become your joys, his sorrows become yours. And the beauty is that when shared, joys double while sorrows halve. If your neighbour buys a Mercedes, instead of burning up with envy, you can share his joy as if it were yours. Yet be relieved of the cost of maintaining it and the worry that it may be stolen! Isn't it wonderful, enjoying the thrill of a Mercedes without having to pay the price!

If you identify with all Indians, you feel excited when any Indian does well. For instance when a Sabeer Bhatia sells his company to Microsoft for US$ 400 million, if you identify with him you feel that you have 400 million dollars in your bank! This is the power of identification, of love. What is the price you have to pay to achieve that state where you enjoy millions without going through the turmoil of making them? Just love.

Most importantly, desires drop. When you identify with others, you give priority to their joys and sorrows. Like Oliver Goldsmith says in 'The Village Preacher' you become 'more skilled to raise the wretched than to rise'. When your accent is on improving the lot of the needy you are not feeding your desires, so they drop.

CELEBRATE EVERY MOMENT

When you have the feeling of gratitude towards that Power, every moment becomes a celebration, you are in rapturous ecstasy all the time. You have the confidence that whatever you need will be given by that Power. You don't need to worry about it, you don't need to ask for it, you don't even need to wonder when or how you will get it. Untouched by life's uncertainties, you are never discouraged, never disheartened. So if you are despondent it is because you lack this spirit and need to inculcate the feeling of gratitude.

CONTROLLED EMOTION

It is important to remember that all emotions need to be under the control of the intellect. Otherwise, even a positive emotion results in devastation. There is a story of a doting mother who could never bring herself to discipline her wayward son. She ignored every fault of his. He grew up thinking that he could get away with anything. Eventually he became a criminal. When he was sentenced to jail, he requested the judge to sentence his mother as well, since she was also responsible for his going astray.

Hence even if the emotion is positive, it needs intellectual guidance.

Bhakti is a well-controlled emotion. Oliver Goldsmith explains this in 'The Village Preacher'.

> 'To them, his heart, his love, his griefs were given,
> But all his serious thoughts had rest in heaven.
> As some tall cliff that lifts its awful form,
> Swells from the vale and midway leaves the storm;
> Though round its breast the rolling clouds are spread,
> Eternal sunshine settles on its head.'

This is the crucial difference. Interact freely with people emotionally but your intellect must be rooted in the higher. Can you picture a tall mountain rising from the valley and enveloped in clouds midway? Above the clouds the air is clear and the peak is ever exposed to sunshine. Similarly the mind feels love but the intellect is not clouded by the love. The intellect is always in touch with the sun above, *Ātman.*

Emotion you must have but **the expression of the emotion must be guided by the intellect.** This is the most important part of *Bhakti.*

Jñāna Yoga

Vedānta means the end of knowledge. It is the knowledge of life and living. This is the path of *Jñāna Yoga.* If you don't have this knowledge, you will make mistakes, some of which may be irredeemable. The human being is blessed with two things which no other species has:

1. Choice of action. All other creatures have to tread a predetermined path. The human being alone is endowed with a choice. With this choice you can evolve to the highest perfection, or sink to the depths of degradation.

2. Intellect. To help make this choice you have the intellect. If you use the intellect to make the right choices you can evolve. Unfortunately what happens in life is that you make choices with a poorly developed intellect. You don't know what to choose in life. As a result you make disastrous choices and end up with regret, remorse and

guilt. The Bhagavad Gītā reinforces the intellect, gives knowledge with which you can make the right choices.

THE RIGHT CHOICE

This choice is difficult because in life sorrow comes in the guise of pleasure, and true happiness appears as sorrow. Anything that gives instant pleasure invariably ends up as permanent sorrow. And vice versa. This has been spelt out in the Gītā. In Chapter 18 Kṛṣṇa tells Arjuna, "True happiness is like poison in the beginning but is nectarine in the end. That which is like nectar in the beginning and poisonous in the end is false happiness."

Go back to your own experiences and find out. Tasty food is pleasurable in the beginning, but it results in ill health. Hence it is called 'junk' food. To miss class and have fun is very pleasant in the beginning, but later on in life the student finds it sorrowful because he is not assured of a good career. To study regularly is painful in the beginning but in the end it gives happiness. A little investment in the study of the Gītā may be difficult initially, but it will yield permanent happiness. Out of sheer ignorance we opt for instant joys and sign up for permanent sorrow in the end. So it is important to know what to choose in life.

HAPPINESS – A STATE OF MIND

We have many misconceptions which lead to wrong action. For instance, where does happiness lie? Most of us believe that happiness lies in external acquisition and enjoyment. The fact of the matter is that happiness lies within. It is a state of mind. And has nothing to do with the external world. You could be in the worst of situations and be happy. You could be miserable in the best environment.

Looking for happiness in the world is like a fly trying to find its way out through a closed window. It struggles and uses up the last of its energies in a futile effort to break through the window. While the open door is just two feet away! All the fly has to do is to put in a fraction of the effort that is now being wasted and it will be liberated from its self-imposed prison. But it has got so locked on to the idea that this is the only way out that it pursues it to the bitter end.

Human effort to find happiness is exactly like that. We are totally misled by ignorance, therefore the need for knowledge. What kind of knowledge? There are laws that govern our functioning and we need to understand and abide by them. Instead we try to gain a secure future by following all kinds of methods. We go to palmists, astrologers, *tāntriks* etc. Nobody can **predict** your future. Only you can **create** it. You can design your future by putting in the right action in the present. The law is that every action has an equal and opposite reaction. In life you get what you deserve, not what you desire. So it is totally redundant to desire. Instead, if you conserve the energy that you are wasting in desiring and redirect it to right action, the result has to come to you. This is how you create a bright future and achieve your goal.

FORBIDDEN FRUIT: DESERVE Vs DESIRE

There is a poem 'The Pineapple and the Bee' by William Cowper which speaks of desire. The poet sees a freshly baked pineapple pudding kept near a window to cool. There is a glass case over it. A bee passing by happens to see the pudding. It is attracted by it and tries its best to break through the glass and get to the pudding. But alas the glass is 'only pervious to the light'. The poet says, 'Thus having wasted half the day, he trims his flight another way'. From what he sees, the poet makes a philosophical observation:

> 'Methinks, I said, in thee I find
> The sin and madness of mankind'.

Sin because it upsets the mind, madness because it is foolish to desire what you do not deserve. The pineapple pudding is meant for the human being, not for the bee. The bee doesn't deserve it.

The poem goes on:

> 'To joys forbidden man aspires,
> Consumes his soul with vain desires,
> Folly the spring of his pursuit
> And disappointment all the fruit.'

When you long for joys you do not deserve, the starting point of your pursuit is foolishness and the outcome is bitter disappointment.

Then he describes the two main motivations that drive a human being in the world: wealth and woman, signifying acquisition and enjoyment. Exactly what Ādi Śaṅkarācārya wrote almost a millennium earlier. A young man sees a beautiful lady go past in a chariot. He wants to meet her but can't. The poet says:

'She is the pineapple, and he
The silly, unsuccessful, bee.'

A young lady goes shopping. She is enthralled with the merchandise displayed but realises she has no money to buy the objects.

'The maid who views with pensive air,
The show glass fraught with glittering ware,
Sees watches, trinkets, rings and lockets
But sighs at the thought of empty pockets;
Like thine, her appetite is keen,
But ah, the cruel glass between!'

There is always that cruel glass standing between you and the object of your desire. It will remain as long as you don't deserve it. Then he goes on to say:

'Our dear delights are often such,
Exposed to view but not to touch,
The sight our foolish heart inflames,
We long for pineapples in frames.'

There are three types of people who approach the problem in different ways. 'With hopeless wish one looks and lingers'. He doesn't do anything, just indulges in wishful thinking. The second one 'Breaks the glass and cuts his fingers.' He goes all out to obtain the object of desire but all that happens is that he gets hurt.

'But they whom truth and wisdom lead
Can gather honey from a weed.'

In chapter III of the Bhagavad Gītā Kṛṣṇa says the same thing. Those who eat the remnants of sacrifice get the fruit, but he who goes after the world with a selfish desire 'cooks but eats sin'. Those who work for spiritual evolution get prosperity as a by-product. The fruit of their effort is sweet. They enjoy it. But a person who is selfish, who puts in a lot of effort, gets only mental agitation. The fruit of selfishness is sorrow.

TRUE KNOWLEDGE – SIEVE THE PERMANENT FROM THE IMPERMANENT

The core of *jñāna*, knowledge, is not academic brilliance, mastery of the Vedas, Upaniṣads or Bhagavad Gītā. In Śaṅkarācārya's words *jñāna* is 'reflection upon the difference between the permanent and the impermanent'.

Wordsworth says,

> "The wise man, I affirm,
> Can find no rest in that which perishes,
> Nor will he lend his heart to aught which doth on time depend...
> But in chaste hearts, uninfluenced by the power of outward change,
> There blooms a deathless flower
> That breathes on earth the air of Paradise."

An academician may or may not have true knowledge, while an illiterate person may have it. Some of the greatest of saints have come from humble backgrounds but have had this unique insight. It has to do with inner perception, the ability to see the difference between the real and the unreal, that which is permanent and that which perishes, the world and the realm beyond. As you reflect upon this, what is an abstract possibility becomes a distinct reality. *Ātman*, which is just a vague concept in your mind today is converted into an intimate becoming. This is the result of knowledge.

REFLECTION – KEY TO WISDOM

Knowledge is not to be skimmed through superficially, learned and parroted. The purpose is to reflect upon it, so that it becomes crystal clear and you live it. Svāmī Rāma Tīrtha gives this example. Glass is made of sand, which is opaque. Yet when sand is processed in a particular way it becomes clear transparent glass. Similarly, the body, mind and intellect are opaque. They block your vision of *Ātman*. With the knowledge of Vedānta you can make the opaque body, mind and intellect transparent so that you see through them and zero in on the core which is *Ātman*.

If you hold your finger in front of your eyes and focus on it, the world that is beyond gets totally blurred. If you focus on the background the solid, opaque finger appears transparent.

So the question is: where is your attention? On the world? Then *Ātman* is out of focus. Shift your concentration to *Ātman* and the world recedes into the background.

There is a saying:

> 'A man that looks on glass,
> On it may stay his eye,
> But if he chooseth, through it pass
> And then the heaven espy.'

The very same world that you are now living in, view it from a different perspective. Then you will see the play of Divinity.

> Elizabeth Browning puts it eloquently:
> 'Earth's crammed with heaven,
> And every common bush afire with God.'

WHO ARE YOU?

When you refer to your body, mind and intellect you say 'my' body, 'my' mind, 'my' intellect. When you use the word 'my' it automatically means that you are different from the body, mind and intellect. Just as when you say 'my' dog you are different from the dog! So if the body, mind and intellect are different from you, then who are you? The word 'personality' comes from the Latin word '*persona*' which means mask. If your personality is a mask, then who are you?

You experience three states of consciousness – waking, dream and deep sleep. In the waking state you say, 'I am the waker'. In the dream state you are a totally different person. But you think it is the same. In the waking state you may have gone through surgery but in the dream, you could be in the pink of health! Thus the dreamer and the waker are not the same. And when you are fast asleep, you experience nothingness. That nothingness is not the dreamer, the dreamer is not the waker and the waker is not nothingness. Yet in all three states of consciousness you say 'I'.

The waker, dreamer and deep sleeper are assumed identities. They are not real because anything that is real endures. What is real is the 'I', but unfortunately you are not able to stay with it. You limit the 'I' by saying I am the waker, I am the dreamer, etc. And you get caught up with the limitations that you impose on yourself. If only you could capture that 'I' without the add-ons, you would achieve Realisation.

This may seem abstract and subtle. But if you invest a little time and effort it helps you become objective. You understand that this world and all that it has to offer is only temporary and passing. You give it the value it deserves. Today there is a premium on it because you assume wrongly that everything in the world is permanent. Nothing in the world endures. If you make the mistake of selling your soul to the world which is fleeting, you will suffer the same fate as Sītā did in the Rāmāyaṇa.

FOCUS ON ĀTMAN

Sītā was blissful in the palace at Ayodhyā as well as in the forest undergoing the rigours of *vanavās* because her mind was absorbed in Rāma – *Ātman.* When her attention was distracted by the golden deer she was taken captive by Rāvaṇa. The deer represents sense objects which are tantalising but ephemeral. Rāvaṇa is the ten-headed monster who symbolises the ten senses.

When your focus shifts from *Ātman* to the world, you are held captive by the ten sense organs. If you maintain the right relationship with sense objects and retain control over them even while enjoying them, you are at peace. This is the trait of a person of knowledge.

TRUE CONVERGENCE

You see the world of diversity. All objects are distinct and different from one another. You hear different sounds. Then you smell, taste and touch a whole variety of objects. You feel myriad emotions, think millions of thoughts. These are also diverse. But in and through your transactions with the world if your focus is on that Power which enables you to perceive all this then that is true knowledge. Knowledge is the ability to trace back all experiences to that one Entity, your own Self, which is also the hub of the Universe. Convergence is not a new concept, it is an age-old reality. The Self is the network of the cosmos.

REVEL IN THE DIVINE

Develop the perception, the *jñāna cakṣu* or eye-of-wisdom, to see the play of Divinity in the world. The permanent through the impermanent, the unity in the diversity. Retrace all your experiences to that one, indivisible Reality. Then you will never get carried away by what you see. Whether beautiful or unattractive, it will not affect you. Because you revel in the thought of that which facilitates your vision.

You hear both pleasant and unpleasant sounds. As long as your focus is on what you hear you get tossed around by what you hear. If your focus moves to that which empowers you to hear then you are in a state of constant exaltation. When you are dealing with difficult people, switch on to this thought. Then the sharper the words hurled at you the greater will be your joy!

So also with emotions. People bombard you with positive as well as negative emotions. You celebrate the positive and mourn the negative. Shift your attention to that which facilitates the feeling and you become immune to people and their influence.

Similarly with thoughts. The world presents you with ideas that are in consonance with your convictions and those that are not. If you focus on the enabling Power, neither affects you.

Why get tossed around by the fluctuations in the external world? In the clamour and trials of the world gain the capacity to retreat into an oasis of peace and happiness. This fantastic capability is *Jñāna Yoga.*

With the practice of *Jñāna Yoga* you become:

- Successful because you have clarity of thinking.
- Happy in any circumstances, because your focus is on the permanent.
- Free from desire because the spiritual desire displaces all desires pertaining to the world.

OVERVIEW: THE THREE *YOGAS*

Over the last few pages, we have discussed the three *yogas* – *karma yoga, bhakti yoga* and *jñāna yoga.* These three spiritual disciplines are mandatory for any spiritual practitioner. The practice lies in changing attitudes, mindsets and motivations. In a nutshell, we can sum up the essential ingredients of the three *yogas* as follows:

Karma Yoga is to find satisfaction, fulfilment, in giving rather than taking. In dedicating yourself to a higher ideal and chanelling all your activities towards that ideal. To focus on contributing to the whole rather than claiming exclusive privileges for yourself. Then you elevate the most menial of tasks to worship.

Bhakti Yoga is a feeling of oneness and love, not only for humanity but also for all living beings. It is the capacity to see yourself in others. When you see your reflection in the mirror, you don't feel any competitiveness towards that image, no sense of 'otherness' towards it. You identify with that image, feel no alienation or threat from it. When this feeling is extended to all other beings it is *Bhakti Yoga.* If you don't see this connection you feel competitive, insecure, threatened by the presence of others. The power of *bhakti* is described by R.W. Emerson in 'Brahma':

> 'The strong gods pine for my abode
> And pine in vain the sacred seven.
> But thou, meek lover of the good,
> Find me, and turn thy back on heaven.'

Jñāna Yoga is the ability to see unity in diversity. To recognise the existence of the same divine Power in all of us. Without this, we feel separate, insecure. We want uniformity. We are uncomfortable with people who are different. The ability to see the unifying thread that binds us all together is *Jñāna Yoga*.

RENUNCIATION

When you practice these three *yogas* concurrently, in proportion to your own composition, you reach the state of renunciation. Renunciation is not to be practised. It is the result of spiritual exercises. When you perform the three *yogas* you reach the exalted state of renunciation. The word renunciation is frightening to most people because they associate it with giving up all the things that are dear to them. Renunciation is the capacity to evaluate correctly the world and all that it contains. When you understand the true worth of everything in the world then you are said to be a person of renunciation. Renunciation is not giving up things. It is understanding their value whether you possess and enjoy them or not.

Nothing communicates better the spirit of renunciation than a poem by Theodore Tilten. It is about a king in Persia who had carved the words 'Even This Will Pass Away' on a signet ring. Mind you, the king did not give up any of his pleasures.

'Once in Persia reigned a king.
Who upon a signet ring
Carved a maxim strange and wise,
When held before his eyes,
Gave him counsel at a glance,
Fit for every change and chance.
Solemn words, and these were they
"Even This Will Pass Away".

Trains of camels through the sand,
Brought him gems from Samarkand;
Fleets of galleys over the seas
Brought him pearls to rival these,
But he counted little gain,
Treasures of the mine or main;
"What is wealth?" the king would say
"Even This Will Pass Away".'

It is not that you have to give up wealth. You only have to understand that wealth will come, only to pass away and if you understand this, you are a person of renunciation. What is the attitude that most of us have towards wealth? We exaggerate its value and strive hard to acquire it, believing it will be with us permanently. It comes only to go, and we must understand this while we have it, not after losing it. This applies to wealth in every sense of the term, not just to money. For instance, it applies to wealth in terms of capabilities as well. Today you have expertise in a particular field so you command respect in society. Tomorrow you may not have it and you will lose that respect. You must be prepared for it.

Then the poem goes on:

'Mid the pleasures of his court
At the zenith of their sport,
When the palms of all his guests
Burned with clapping at his jests,
Seated midst the figs and wine,
Said the king: "Ah, friends of mine,
Pleasure comes but not to stay
"Even This Will Pass Away".'

While he enjoys the fame and popularity bestowed on him, he remains aware of their transitory nature. Then the king gets married:

'Woman fairest ever seen
Was the bride he crowned as queen,
Pillowed on the marriage-bed
Whispering to his soul, he said,
Though no monarch ever pressed
Fairer bosom to his breast,
Mortal flesh is only clay!
"Even This Will Pass Away".'

So it is an internal understanding, not an external expression.

Then he is injured while fighting in a battlefield and when he is brought back bleeding he tells himself:

'Pain is hard to bear,
But with patience day by day
"Even This Will Pass Away".'

What is the difference between an ordinary person and a famous person? The ordinary person fades into oblivion after a few days. A famous person is remembered for many years after his death. That's the only difference.

'Towering in a public square
Forty cubits in the air,
And the king disguised, unknown
Gazed upon his sculptured name,
And he pondered, "What is fame?"
Fame is but a slow decay!
"Even This Will Pass Away".'

If you lead a life of renunciation, you find that you are able to meet death with the same fortitude with which you faced all the other challenges in life:

'Struck with palsy, sore and old,
Waiting at the gates of gold,
Said he with his dying breath
"Life is done, but what is death"?
Then as answer to the king
Fell a sunbeam on his ring

Showing by a heavenly ray,
"Even This Will Pass Away".'

PHYSICAL PLEASURES FOUND WANTING

Renunciation is growing to something more meaningful, more gratifying, and more fulfilling. When you contact a sense object, no doubt it gives you a certain amount of joy. But that is not all the happiness that you are entitled to. As a human being you have the capacity to access higher and more fulfilling levels of satisfaction.

EMOTIONAL JOYS MORE FULFILLING

If you taste the joy of emotional gratification, you will find it far superior to physical pleasure. Take the example of Sudhā, a young maid. She works day and night, stretches herself beyond physical limits to work for the welfare of her children. She looks years older than her age because of the tough life she has led. She sometimes brings her children to the home that she is working in and her employer remarks that they are well dressed, well educated and well mannered. It gladdens Sudhā's heart. She gloats over the fact that her children are doing well. She doesn't feel the sacrifice. She only experiences the higher joy, the emotional thrill. So what happens when you rise from the physical to the emotional level is that physical appetites and desires do not bother you. They recede.

THE THRILL OF INTELLECTUAL PURSUITS

Then you rise still higher to an intellectual ideal. Doctors go for days without rest or sleep, fired with the goal of using their medical knowledge to save lives. Scientists working on path-breaking research have no record of day or night, meals or rest, family or friends. The joy and exhilaration they feel has no equal among emotional or physical joys.

WELCOME TO THE REALM OF THE INFINITE

Can you imagine the power of a spiritual ideal? It is truly Infinite. Nothing else matters. Even mathematically, we know that infinite remains infinite irrespective of anything added to or subtracted from it:

Infinite + Infinite = Infinite
Infinite – Infinite = Infinite

You reach that state of total fulfilment from which nothing can be taken away or enhanced. It remains permanently yours.

There is a fascinating story of Sudāmā and Kṛṣṇa. Sudāmā, a dear childhood friend of Kṛṣṇa's, had lived in poverty all his life. One day Sudāmā's wife asks him to request Kṛṣṇa for a little help. Sudāmā agrees. He remembers that Kṛṣṇa is very fond of beaten rice, *pohā*. So he asks his wife to make some *pohā* for Kṛṣṇa. What a beautiful thought! He is going to Kṛṣṇa to ask for help yet all he can think of is giving. This is the state of fulfilment. Sudāmā goes to meet Kṛṣṇa who is delighted to see him. They bask in each other's company and after a few days Sudāmā bids goodbye and returns without having asked for help! When he gets home, he finds his humble cottage replaced by a lavish mansion with all the comforts and luxuries befitting a king!

When you are gripped with a spiritual ideal, when you understand that your role in life here is only to get to that state of Realisation, you become indifferent to physical, emotional as well as intellectual joys.

Renunciation is not life-denying. It is life-enabling. It is an exhilarating confidence in a higher mission. As you rise to the higher, not only do you have access to the higher joys you also enjoy the lower ones. So it's a win-win situation. Let us examine our lives. Most of our enjoyments are restricted to the physical plane. But we indulge in them unintelligently and the law of diminishing returns comes into force. With every succeeding contact the enjoyment reduces till finally it comes down to zero. At that point it ceases to yield joy but we still have to maintain contact because denial brings sorrow. Thus we end up in a situation where having the good things of life gives no happiness but denial brings sorrow. This leads to depression. Is it surprising that Prozac, an anti-depressant, is the highest selling medicine in the US? Renunciation gives back enjoyment to you. It restores the joy of living. It does not deprive anyone of his or her joys.

No adult is happy denying a child the pleasure of playing with toys. But every adult is interested in the child growing to appreciate things far more fulfilling than toys. Similarly no spiritual master wants to deny us our toys – wealth, position, fame, power – and so on. But every spiritual master calls us to more fulfilling avenues of happiness. Till finally you taste the joy of the Spirit – the state of spiritual adulthood.

FOCUS GETS YOU THERE

There is a story of an old king who had no heir. He devised a unique method to select the future king. He organised a large amusement park. The king would be present in the park, but in disguise, and the person who could recognise him would be the next king. It seemed simple enough, but when people entered the park they got so involved in the entertainment provided that they forgot the purpose for which they had entered it. The trivial exhibits were so attractive that they enthralled them. They totally forgot about the king and the fact that they had come there only to find him! This happened day after day until one day a smart young man entered the amusement park. Like the others he also enjoyed what the park had to offer. But simultaneously he looked in every nook and corner for the king. He never lost sight of the fact that he had to spot him. Having searched everywhere he was tired and exhausted. He sat in the only permanent structure there. Just as he was about to conclude that the king was nowhere on the premises, he realised he was sitting near a small temple. There was a *pujārī* (priest) doing *ārati* (worship) and he was attracted by the bell. Suddenly he realised that this was the one place where he had not looked for the king. He asked the *pujārī* to turn around. Lo and behold there was the king! He had found him.

The world is one big amusement park and we have gained entry here only to claim kingship. But this world is so attractive, so tempting, so tantalising, that we get stuck somewhere or the other and completely forget the mission for which we have come into the world. The person who keeps that mission in mind and goes through the motions of life is a person of renunciation. Because whatever he does, wherever he goes, whoever he contacts, it is only for this purpose. As long as you understand this and go through with your actions in life, you are safe, you are secure. But when you lose track of this, you are lost. And all of us are completely lost in the world. We don't know for what reason we have come into this world, we don't know what we are doing here or where we are headed. We just exist from day to day. And we get involved and distracted by the petty, trivial things of life that perturb and disturb us. But if we are able to maintain that focus even for a little while during the day, it makes a great difference to our lives.

ACTION IN RENUNCIATION

Renunciation is not giving up action, it is acting in a spirit of renunciation. The first verse in Chapter VI of the Bhagavad Gītā describes a *sannyāsī*, a perfect person. A *sannyāsī* is one who acts without depending on the fruit of action. He does what he ought to do, renouncing the *karmaphala* or fruit of action. It is the anxiety for the fruit of action, the craving and passion backing the action, that impede your progress. If you are able to drop these and just act, you perform perfect action. You get to the exalted state of a *sannyāsī*. But you are constantly plagued by desire pushing you from the past and anxiety for the fruit pulling you from the future. As a result your mind is never in the present.

When it is hot and humid outside, it saps you of energy. Whereas when it is pleasant and humidity levels are low, you have far greater stamina. The heat and humidity are like desire and ego within us. Desire and ego impede action, retard performance. Once you knock off desire and ego you perform to your optimum capacity.

RENOUNCE AND ENJOY

As a home or office that is not maintained well gets cluttered with all kinds of useless objects, the mind too is burdened with negative thoughts. Meaningless and routine activities clog the mind and dissipate energy. Renunciation is clearing out the cobwebs, getting rid of the debris which clutters your mind and prevents you from concentrating on that which is important.

Vedānta implores you to enjoy life by giving up that which interrupts your happiness. Your happiness is periodically interspersed with bouts of sorrow. It is this sorrow that you have to renounce. Desire, attachment, craving and ego are the culprits that cause sorrow. Renounce these and enjoy life. Renunciation transforms your life from that of mediocrity to one of excellence, from drudgery to revelry, indignation to inspiration. Vedānta invites you to experience the magic of life.

MEDITATION

With renunciation you become meditative by nature. Your mind is withdrawn from the world. It is not chasing after things of the world. When that mind which is withdrawn from external preoccupations is available to you, you are able to focus it on one thought, expelling all others under the watchful eye of the intellect. This is called meditation. When you meditate, you repeat a *mantra* or word-symbol. During meditation the mind repeats the *mantra,* the intellect observes it. The intellect is distinguishing between sound (*mantra*) and silence which is called *amātrā.* When you focus on that one thought for a period of time you stop the *mantra.* The thought flow stops and the mind ceases to exist because the mind is nothing but a flow of thoughts. The sound goes, only silence remains. The intellect whose function is to differentiate between sound and silence finds that there is no pair to discriminate between. So the intellect also becomes extinct. When the mind and intellect are gone what remains is *Ātman.* You attain Self Realisation. When you reach that stage of Realisation, you are called a *sthitaprajña.* A Perfect Person.

Bhagavad Gītā Chapter II

Verses 54 to 72

PROFILE OF THE PERFECT PERSON

This is one of the most popular portions of the Bhagavad Gītā. In fact, this is where the Gītā really begins. The first chapter and initial ten verses of the second chapter detail Arjuna's dilemma, grief and ultimate breakdown. It is only when he completely surrenders to Kṛṣṇa and seeks his guidance that Kṛṣṇa speaks.

Verses 11 to 53 of Chapter II, however, give the highest philosophy. More therapeutic than educative, they are designed to shake Arjuna out of his stupor and make him more receptive to the knowledge that follows. It is also an assurance to Arjuna that Kṛṣṇa is not only a friend willing to help in a crisis. He is more, far more. Kṛṣṇa has the awesome wisdom to lead Arjuna out of delusion and inaction to the pinnacle of Perfection.

Arjuna shows signs of partial awakening when he asks a question in verse 54. This, however, is not relevant to his particular situation. Nevertheless, Kṛṣṇa meticulously answers the question. By this time Arjuna's recovery is complete.

Verse 54

अर्जुन उवाच
स्थितप्रज्ञस्य का भाषा समाधिस्थस्य केशव।
स्थितधीः किं प्रभाषेत किमासीत व्रजेत किम् ॥ ५४ ॥

Arjuna uvāca
Sthitaprajñasya kā bhāṣā samādhisthasya Keśava
Sthitadhīḥ kiṁ prabhāṣeta kimāsīta vrajeta kim

Arjuna said:
O Keśava, what is the definition of a *sthitaprajña* (one established in Wisdom), absorbed in *samadhi* (meditation)? How does one rooted in Wisdom speak, sit, walk?

We all look for role models. Someone to look up to, to emulate; someone who has walked the path before us. Someone who has 'made it' in life. In today's world, the role models seem to be the rich and famous. In contrast Arjuna understands that it is only internal enrichment that makes for true success. Therefore he asks for the definition of a perfect Person.

Most of us have either a hazy or distorted idea of Perfection. Externally you may not be able to tell a perfect Person from the rest of humanity. But there is a world of difference internally. We have no access to his inner state and make the mistake of assessing him by superfluous parameters. Consequently we go completely wrong, conferring Divinity on ordinary people and ascribing mediocrity to outstanding sages! We lead ourselves up the garden path. Hence it is imperative to have an accurate benchmark of Perfection. So that we know which direction to move in and which role model to emulate.

Arjuna is confused. Realised Persons across time have exhibited varied characteristics. Some were gregarious while others lived as recluses. Some enjoyed lavish lifestyles while others thrived on austerity. Arjuna is not sure what makes for Perfection. And which of the external expressions he should follow.

Arjuna's question consists of four parts:

1. *Kā bhāṣā* — What is the profile of a perfect Person?
2. *Kiṁ āsīta* — How does he sit? What goes on inside him?

What is it that sets the perfected One apart from the rest of us? In questions 1 and 2 Arjuna wants an insight into the inner personality of a realised Person. What makes him tick? How does it feel to break free from all limitations and live in the state of Infinity?

3. *Kiṁ prabhāṣeta* – How does he speak? Speech is a metonym indicating all organs of action. How does he act?
4. *Kiṁ vrajeta* – How does he walk? How does he connect with the world?

Here Arjuna asks — how does his inner revelation impact on his interaction with the world? How does he network with the world? Having reached the Infinite status, how does he reconcile it with the finitude of the world?

Hence it is a complete question seeking the illustration of a person of Excellence. The subsequent verses communicate the depth of the human personality, incomprehensible to the common person. Yet the masterly presentation is such that anyone can understand, relate to and strive to emulate.

Arjuna asks Kṛṣṇa about the highest level of Perfection in a human being. In the next verse, Kṛṣṇa gives the definition of a realised Person. In verses 56-59, He expounds on the definition with greater descriptive clarity. In verse 60 He talks about how the powerful senses attack the mind and lead it astray. In verses 61-66 He gives the pivotal role of the intellect. In 67 He says that the mind which has been misled by the senses drags the intellect away. And when your intellect goes, He emphatically says, you perish. In verse 68 He says only a person who has controlled the senses qualifies to be a *sthitaprajña*. Verses 69-72 bring out the conclusion.

Verse 55

श्रीभगवानुवाच
प्रजहाति यदा कामान्सर्वान्पार्थ मनोगतान् ।
आत्मन्येवात्माना तुष्टः स्थितप्रज्ञस्तदोच्यते ॥ ५५ ॥

Śrī Bhagavan uvāca
Prajahāti yadā kāmānsarvān Pārtha manogatān
Ātmanyevātmanā tuṣṭaḥ sthitaprajñastadocyate

The blessed Lord said
O Pārtha (son of Pṛtha), when all desires of the mind are totally abandoned and one is fulfilled in the Self alone by the Self, then one is said to be a *sthitaprajña* (one established in Wisdom).

Pārtha is another name for Arjuna, meaning son of Pṛtha, Kuntī. Throughout the Bhagavad Gītā, both Kṛṣṇa and Arjuna address each other by various names. Apart from lending a poetic charm to the text, it indicates the tremendous love they have for each other. This is essential for any communication, especially spiritual. Subtle, abstract concepts are understood better when there is affection and confidence between teacher and student.

Here Kṛṣṇa gives two attributes that make for Perfection. Irrespective of one's lifestyle, race or nationality as long as one develops these attributes, one is a *sthitaprajña*. The qualifications are given in the positive as well as in the negative. He first gives the negative aspect because it is easier to understand. A person of steady wisdom is one who totally abandons all desires from the mind. That sounds frightening to us. Then Kṛṣṇa follows it up with a positive assertion to complete the picture. He has no desires because he is fulfilled in the Self alone by the Self. Self means *Ātman*. *Ātman* is the absolute state of Godhood. When you have access to your own Infinite status, everything else pales into insignificance. The value of all finite things instantly comes down to zero. He is giving us a definition in the absolute. It is impossible to understand the absolute. Hence we must come down to our level. Understand its meaning with reference to our life and then extrapolate to understand what He is talking about.

Kṛṣṇa is referring to growth — the escalation from one state of preoccupation to another. We have all been through some form of growth. Today you are an adult but at some point of time you were a child. From childhood till adulthood, you went through various stages of development. At each stage you were gripped with desires pertaining to that level. For example as an infant your whole life revolved around your mother. As a toddler, toys were your world. Then you encountered the thrill of computer games and got hooked onto the computer. You very graciously gave the toys away to your younger brother, who was bowled over by your sense of renunciation! And one fine day you found computer games also didn't enthrall you. Why? You'd fallen in love! Thus you grew into a full-fledged adult. Now you are engrossed in 'adult' attractions – career, family, home etc.

This is how you escalate to higher desires. When you are captivated by a higher interest, your previous desires fade away. Having reached adulthood, all you want to do is maintain status quo. But there are miles to go. If you can visualise something beyond what the world has to offer you gain that perspective which will motivate you to move even higher.

This is portrayed in Plato's metaphor. A community of people lives in a cave for generations. A smart young man from among them once gets inspired and tells the others, "Look, there must be something beyond this cave. The whole universe cannot be just this little dwelling place. Let us explore." The others have never considered this possibility and are unwilling to accommodate the thought. So they dissuade him from pursuing with the matter. Confused but obedient, he follows their advice. But after a few days that restlessness again arises within him. He is now convinced that there must be something beyond the cave and he knows that nobody else shares his view.

So he decides to explore. He sets out by himself. Soon he finds he is in total darkness. He no longer has the comforting light of the settlement. He has not reached the mouth of the cave either. He is neither here nor there. Now that's a frightening condition to be in. But his conviction that there has to be a world beyond the cave keeps him going. He walks on until he sees a faint light glimmering in the distance. This is the new world beckoning him. His confidence grows and he continues his pursuit with renewed vigour. He finally reaches the mouth of the cave.

He comes out into the open and experiences the magnificent world we take for granted — the brilliant sun, the refreshing water, the gentle breeze, the infinite expanse of sky and sea, the majestic mountains, the breathtaking splash of colours, the mind-blowing variety of flowers and fruits, birds and beasts….. He is overwhelmed with joy. He basks in his newfound experience for a couple of days. Then he thinks of his family and community in the cave. He decides to go back and bring them out.

He goes with enthusiasm. He is elated since he has experienced the truth and cannot wait to share it with the others. Back in the cave, he speaks with greater conviction — he describes the beautiful world out there. How do you think his elders react? They look at each other and say, "We always knew there was something not quite right with him". Because he speaks a language they do not understand. When he describes the sun and stars, they have no idea what he is talking about. So they think he is mad.

Plato beautifully captures the essence of the spiritual journey in this metaphor. There is that inner call of the Divine in all of us which tells us that there has to be something beyond the life we know. And there is the exploratory spirit in us. When you embark on this journey you find that nobody is with you. People mock you for your convictions and sometimes act as hindrances in your path to discovering the truth. They think that you are lost when in fact they are the ones who are lost! Once you are able to pursue the truth alone, you reach a state where you are out of sync with other people but you have not yet experienced the higher. You can no longer be content with worldly pleasures but you have no access to spiritual joys. You are in no-man's land. However you must persevere nevertheless. Then you get an indication that you are on the right track. Things start going right in your life. You gain the unshakeable confidence that you are on the right path. With this renewed conviction you continue till you reach Realisation.

In India a great seer has emerged in each generation to speak to us of the new world — the experience of the fourth plane of Consciousness. But since we do not understand, we wonder what he is speaking of. Why should he come back and speak to us? He has no other intention but to share the bliss and serenity of his experience. He tells us the Truth. Initially you may not comprehend the message of the scriptures, but over time you realise its veracity. This is the *guru-śiṣya paramparā* — the mentor-*protégé* lineage which has continued from the beginning of time.

Spiritual evolution must be gradual. When you are full of desires you cannot suddenly drop them. In fact you cannot drop desires at all. What you can do is learn to appreciate something of greater value. Something more fulfilling than what you are engaged in right now. Make an intelligent evaluation of the pleasures available to you. Understand that there are subtler aspects within which give far greater happiness. Then you will no longer be swayed by the lower joys. If you are at the physical level, try and move up to the emotional plane. Once you taste the joy of emotional gratification your own erstwhile physical pleasures seem trivial. Escalate to an intellectual goal and even emotional joys fade into insignificance. Finally when the lure of the Infinite grips you nothing in the world will ensnare you. All finite joys lose their lustre in the brilliance of the Infinite. Just as floodlights in a cricket stadium are insignificant in the glare of the midday sun.

This is the positive aspect of the definition of a realised Soul. If Kṛṣṇa had not given this, it would have misled us. If He had said, "When one completely abandons all desires of the mind then one is a realised Soul" all of humanity would qualify. In deep sleep. Because there are no desires in deep sleep. But that is not Realisation because in that state you have no knowledge of the Self or *Ātman*. You must qualify both in the negative and the positive aspects. When all desires of the mind are totally relinquished **as a result of** being satisfied in the Self, then one is said to be rooted in wisdom.

Growth takes place in every aspect. In plants the sap flows up in one direction. Blood pumped by the heart cannot return because of the one-way system of valves in the arteries. Similarly in the systole and diastole of life once you leave an abyss there is no return. We are compelled to obey life's forward impulse. Growth, escalation, is unidirectional. The Gītā gives you this assurance, '*yad gatvā na nivartante*'. Once you get to the higher level you do not regress to the previous stage.

Here in Verse 55 he gives the definition of a Self-realised Person. This is explained in the Bṛhadāraṇyaka Upaniṣad in three words, '*āptakāma, ātmakāma, akāma.*' *Āptakāma* means all desires are fulfilled. This happens when you have *Ātmakama*, the desire for *Ātman*. The lure of the Infinite neutralises all worldly desires. Then you go to the state of *akāma,* desirelessness. This is Realisation.

Verse 56

दुःखेष्वनुद्विग्नमनाः सुखेषु विगतस्पृहः ।
वीतरागभयक्रोधः स्थितधीर्मुनिरुच्यते ॥ ५६ ॥

Duḥkheṣvanudvignamanāḥ sukheṣu vigataspṛhaḥ
Vītarāgabhayakrodhaḥ sthitadhīrmunirucyate

One is said to be a *muni* (sage) rooted in Wisdom when one's mind is not perturbed by sorrow nor does one yearn for joy; one is free from desire, fear and anger.

Two significant words used here are, *sthitadhī* and *muni*. *Sthitadhī* is one of 'steady intellect'. *Muni* means a contemplator, visionary, thinker. A combination of these two is essential for all development, material or spiritual.

Kṛṣṇa answers the question, 'How does he sit?' What is the inner profile of the person of Realisation?

He refers to two things. One is that the mind is not affected by joy or sorrow emanating from within. Many a time, you may find that, even while sitting alone, you feel extremely happy, elated. Yet at other times, there may be sadness within you for no discernable reason. These are various mood fluctuations within. They are a result of the quality of actions you have performed in the past. If, in the past, you have been engaged in unselfish, dedicated actions your mood will be good. But if you have been selfish and negative, then you will go through the lows of life. The problem does not lie in the joy or sorrow. It is in the affectation. Everyone goes through happiness and sadness. They are an inevitable part of life. You cannot have one without the other. Pairs of opposites are inherent in the world, in your mind. But you need not be affected by them.

Mumbaiites will be able to understand this concept from a simple analogy. *Bhel* is a popular snack unique to Mumbai. It is a wonderful mix of different tastes — it is spicy as well as sweet, crisp as well as moist, salty and sour at the same time. What a unique combination of pairs of opposites! And it is this combination of opposites that makes it so enjoyable. You must know how to enjoy the *bhel*. Foreigners are not used to this assault on their taste buds and ask for sweet *bhel*! The *bhel* of life is a mixture of various flavours, different emotions. Relish the flavours of life well but do not get moved by them. Remain an unattached spectator. Then you enjoy the fluctuations of joy and sorrow that come your way.

In the game of life the world is your adversary. To win you must know the rules of the game. And assess the opponent. The world is a sea of change. The Sanskrit word for world is *saṁsāra* — that which changes, comes and goes. To add to your woes the changing world is immune to your control. So you must learn to face the euphoric highs as well as the dismal lows with balance. Accept the world as it is and do not expect any assured pattern. Life is a high-risk venture.

You cannot depend on the vagaries of the world. Otherwise you become a poor loser in the game you have chosen to play!

This does not mean that a perfect Person is indifferent. A plant demonstrates no emotion. An animal on the other hand displays emotion but is swayed by it. And it has no choice but to act on it. Even a well-trained dog will go into a joyful frenzy when its master returns after a long absence. And it will be miserable, sometimes even die, when abandoned. As a human being you have the unique capacity to feel deep emotion, at the same time remain unaffected by it. You act on the sane counsel of the intellect.

The second thing He speaks of is freedom from desire, fear and anger. How does desire come? You think of food only on an empty stomach. When you've had a heavy meal the thought of food doesn't enter your mind. Even if someone offers you your favourite dish, you decline. So the fact that you are plagued by desire implies an emptiness within. Desire emanates from a deficiency. This feeling of deficiency haunts every one, every moment of one's life. The Bhagavad Gītā says that this feeling of emptiness is imaginary. You are not empty at all. You are full, whole, and complete. Totally fulfilled. But for some strange, inexplicable reason you do not know it. And it is this ignorance that is the cause of the whole problem. All your desires spring from that fundamental ignorance of your own completeness. This ignorance is the fertile breeding ground of desire. So when Kṛṣṇa says a realised Soul is free from desire He means he is free from that feeling of emptiness. He has come to understand that he is in fact whole. Full. This is the state of Realisation.

Fear and anger are aberrations of desire. Gratification of desire gives rise to fear of losing what you have acquired. And desire obstructed creates anger. For instance when you acquire a great deal of wealth and the desire for money is satiated, there is fear that someone will take it away – a thief, the government, or perhaps even your spouse! And if you are not able to earn the money there is anger towards the obstruction that prevents you from making the money.

When you are free from desire you are automatically free from fear and anger. The clue here is that if you have a tendency to be fearful or angry it means there are a lot of desires at play. Anger and fear cannot arise without an underlying desire. You need to analyse what you have a desire for and deal with the root of the problem. Then fear and anger will automatically go. Any other method of dealing with these emotions without tackling their root cause, desire, will prove ineffective.

Until such time that you gain the knowledge to conquer desire, fear and anger, the Gītā recommends their management and containment. This is done with the intellect. When the intellect disciplines and directs desire, it becomes far less virulent. Uncontrolled desire is like a deadly virus which devastates and kills. Controlled desire is like the vaccine of the same virus which protects you from infection. It transforms into a goal which triggers achievement and progress in the world.

The intellect removes irrational fears through analysis. And re-deploys anger against evil and injustice. Thus even before you gain knowledge of the Self you are relatively free from the ill effects of desire and its aberrations — fear and anger.

The intellect of a person of steady wisdom is fixed in the Truth. Truth of his fullness. When desire starts bothering you, if you powerfully suggest to yourself that you are whole and that you really do not need this fulfilment, it gives temporary relief. But if you were to gain complete knowledge of your fullness, how wonderfully free you would be!

Verse 57

यः सर्वत्रानभिस्नेहस्तत्तत्प्राप्य शुभाशुभम् ।
नाभिनन्दति न द्वेष्टि तस्य प्रज्ञा प्रतिष्ठिता ॥ ५७ ॥

Yaḥ sarvatrānabhisnehastattatprāpya śubhāśubham
Nābhinandati na dveṣṭi tasya prajñā pratiṣṭhitā

One is established in Wisdom when one is everywhere, unattached; neither elated at obtaining good nor vexed with evil.

In this verse He answers the question, 'How does he walk — *kiṁ vrajeta*?' Meaning, how does he interact with the world? You might wonder after having read the earlier verses, is a realised Person like a piece of stone? What happens to a stone? Whether it is kicked around or worshipped, the stone is indifferent. You might feel that a realised Person is like that.

He elucidates this by saying *yaḥ sarvatra. Yaḥ* means 'any individual'. The Gītā is an all-encompassing science of Perfection applicable to all human beings, at all times. It is not the exclusive domain of Brāhmaṇas, Hindus or even Indians. *Sarvatra* means everywhere. He is on the move, energetic. An epitome of dynamism. He has not withdrawn into seclusion.

Then He puts in a word which sets him apart from the rest of us — *anabhisneha* — unattached. This is the difference between the realised Person and us. He has mastered the art of maintaining physical contact with the world while remaining mentally detached. Whereas you fluctuate between indifference and attachment. There is a third option which you do not know of, which remains unexplored – wholehearted participation in worldly activities with total inner detachment.

This is demonstrated by the innovation of the Post-it note. Its unique feature is that it sticks as long as you want it to stick. And it detaches itself without tearing when you no longer need it. An unattached person is exactly like that. He gives of himself completely to relationships at home, at work and in society. But when the time comes to part he exits gracefully, without heartache or turmoil.

A young man is happy by himself. Then he meets the woman of his dreams. Through constant thinking he gets attached to her. Thereafter when she is away he's miserable. His happiness hinges on her presence. This is attachment. Thus you get attached to various things and people. You cannot move without them. You need an entire entourage wherever you go. You lose your freedom.

There are two problems with attachment. One, you are unhappy even when the contact remains. And two, you lose the object you are attached to. This is the law. Emphatically presented by Svāmī Rāma Tīrtha. A typical example of this is a mother with her child. If she is attached to the child she is in a state of constant anxiety, torment and paranoia even when things are all right. If the child so much as sneezes, she imagines he is getting pneumonia! Every stage of the child's life is traumatic. As a result, the child who is supposed to be a source of joy and happiness to the mother in effect gives only sorrow. And the irony is that everyone else enjoys the child! When she continues like this it results in a negative relationship. The child becomes averse to the mother's mollycoddling. All this is a result of attachment which is nothing but self-love. And any selfishness is repulsive.

A miser is attached to his wealth. He suffers as a result of that attachment. And loses the wealth in the end! Therefore Kṛṣṇa implores you not to get attached. He does not say you should not contact the world. By all means have the world. **But without attachment**. Only then can you enjoy what you have acquired.

The majority of people fluctuate between two categories. Those who contact the world with attachment and suffer. And those who physically keep away from the world in the guise of spirituality and suffer! The latter suffer because they deny themselves things that they are still attached to. Attachment has no connection with physical contact. It is mental dependence. So to remain detached you do not have to sever relationships or physically remove yourself from a person or object. All you need to do is retain your inner independence. When your happiness is not dependent on any object or being you are detached. And detachment can come only when you get attached to the higher, the highest being *Ātman*.

Tat tat prāpya śubha aśubhaṁ na abhinandati na dveṣti — He does not exult at obtaining good nor does he get perturbed by evil. The world consists of pairs of opposites. Comfort and discomfort at the physical realm, elation and desolation at the emotional level, credit and discredit at the intellectual plane. These are inherent in the world. What complicates it is that our system is full of desires. So when something happens in the world that is in sync with our desires we love it, like it, rejoice at it. When external happenings are not in consonance with our desires we hate it. These fluctuations result in a roller coaster ride which is sorrowful.

So how do we get that balance? When you rise above that level to a higher realm. Even temporarily if you are charged emotionally, you are freed from physical ups and downs. Suppose a member of your family has to undergo surgery. You take it upon yourself to take care of him. Your body gets fatigued, you are sleepy etc. but at that time you do not even feel any of it. You can put in hours of gruelling hard work and not feel the strain. You gain freedom from the pairs of opposites at the physical level because you have risen above them to the emotional realm.

When you identify with the intellect both physical and emotional fluctuations do not matter. To a scientist engrossed in research meal times and anniversaries become unimportant.

Ultimately when you identify with *Ātman*, you get total freedom from the fluctuations of the world. You have no interest in the inadequate, passing fancies of the world. It is the nostalgia of the Infinite that beckons you.

We all know that iron by itself is attracted to a magnet, while wood is not. However when iron and wood are firmly bound together, they are attracted to the magnet. Does that mean that the wood is vulnerable to the influence of the magnet? No. The wood remains uninfluenced, pristine.

Your personality is exactly like the wood-iron combination. The wood symbolises *Ātman* while the iron represents the body, mind, intellect. Matter influences matter. The magnetic force of the world is bound to affect the body, mind, intellect. But matter cannot hold sway over Spirit. *Ātman* is ever free. However you are so intricately woven with the matter layers that when the world influences them, you feel victimised. Thus when the good and the evil of the world impact on the material components you get afflicted. And meekly submit to them. You lose the leverage and authority of *Ātman*, your real Self. When the body is ravaged by disease you feel devastated. When fit you feel fine. When the mind is hurt you are sad. When loved you are overjoyed. When the intellect is condemned you are depressed. When admired you are pleased. But even as you feel influenced *Ātman*, the real Self, is untouched. The world does not have the power to influence *Ātman*. All your problems stem from this bondage, attachment with the body, mind and intellect. Shift your focus away from matter to the Self in you. And you will remain unaffected through the oscillations of the world.

This is what Kṛṣṇa is saying in this verse. You must learn the art of withdrawing into the oasis of peace and tranquillity in and through the fluctuations that the body, mind and intellect go through. If you do that you will remain *samam,* balanced. You will neither be elated nor get vexed.

Verse 58

यदा संहरते चायं कूर्मोङ्गानीव सर्वशः ।
इन्द्रियाणीन्द्रियार्थेभ्यस्तस्य प्रज्ञा प्रतिष्ठता ॥ ५८ ॥

Yadā saṁharate cāyaṁ kūrmoṅgāniva sarvaśaḥ
Indriyāṇīndriyārthebhyastasya prajña pratiṣṭhitā

One is established in Wisdom when one restrains one's sense organs from their sense objects, like the tortoise which pulls its limbs back from all sides.

This verse answers the question *'kiṁ prabhāṣeta'?* — How does he speak? Here speech is used metonymically. A metonym is a way of indicating the whole by using a part. For instance he uses speech *(prabhāṣeta)* to indicate all actions performed by the body. To convey it even more lucidly he gives a metaphor. The tortoise is endowed with a hard shell and six appendages which protrude from under the crust. It moves using all its appendages. But faced with mortal danger, it retreats into its protective covering. Then it is safe.

A realised Person has been compared with the tortoise. He engages himself in the world using his six faculties — the five senses and the mind. But as soon as he feels the lure of worldly temptations he withdraws within, under the stronghold of the intellect.

The tortoise's shell represents the realised Person's intellect which is fortified to withstand temptation. Just as the crust is always in contact with the sun above, the intellect of a realised Soul is in constant communion with the Sun above — *Ātman.* It is this alignment that protects him from the assault of the world.

This is the description of the state of Realisation and also a useful tip that we can employ to get there. You should contact the world freely with the senses and mind. However, the intellect should be strong, alert and constantly exposed to the higher values of life. So that when temptation comes your way you are able to withdraw the senses and mind under the secure protection of the intellect.

If you do this, you will be protected from unnecessary detours in the world. However, this is not what people do. They either binge or completely withdraw from the world. Both are unhealthy. You should live life with confidence. This comes as a result of a strong intellect. Then you will be able to handle the temptations of the world.

Even so, most people have one or two weaknesses. When you sense the likelihood of being swept away by your particular weakness withdraw with the help of the intellect. If not you will be in trouble. And all of us are in trouble because we do not apply this formula. So He does not say you should keep away from the world. He only says beware of your particular weaknesses.

Verse 59

विषया विनिवर्तन्ते निराहारस्य देहिनः ।
रसवर्जं रसोऽप्यस्य परं दृष्ट्वा निवर्तते ॥ ५९ ॥

Viṣayā vinivartante nirāhārasya dehinaḥ
Rasavarjaṁ raso'pyasya paraṁ dṛṣṭvā nivartate

When one abstains sense objects recede, but the fondness remains. The fondness goes only on seeing the Supreme.

When a person makes up his mind and abstains from a particular enjoyment, the sense objects themselves seem to recede. But the preference for them remains. This fondness also goes when one Realises.

Here again He gives a valuable hint. If you want to control a weakness, as you make up your mind and exert your will, the object automatically turns away. An overweight person has a tremendous weakness for food. But when she is convinced that she needs to be healthy, the refrigerator shelves automatically empty. When a chain smoker decides to refrain from smoking, not only cigarettes but even ashtrays and lighters seem to vanish from sight.

However the *rasa* or fondness does not go. It lingers until you reach the Supreme. The *rasa* vanishes completely only when you realise the Self. Realisation is infinite happiness. Compared to the infinite all finite entities lose their appeal.

The message is that you have to be attentive and vigilant all the time. Till Realisation, the taste for sense enjoyment lingers. It can surface at any moment and take you away from the path.

The story goes that Pārvatī wanted to marry Lord Śiva, the embodiment of asceticism. She asked for permission to serve him. Śiva accepted her services but married her only after vanquishing Kāmadeva, the god of love. Even Lord Śiva took adequate precaution knowing the power of the senses. In contrast, the modern generation goes headlong into sense indulgence with no thought of inner fortification.

Verse 60

यततो ह्यपि कौन्तेय पुरुषस्य विपश्चितः ।
इन्द्रियाणि प्रमाथीनि हरन्ति प्रसभं मनः ॥ ६० ॥

Yatato hyapi Kaunteya puruṣasya vipaścitaḥ
Indriyāṇi pramāthīni haranti prasabhaṁ manaḥ

The stormy senses violently drag the mind of even a constantly striving wise person, O Kaunteya (son of Kuntī).

Much emphasis is placed on sense control. People embark on the spiritual path with sincerity and commitment, but how many pay attention to sense control? How many people even understand what sense control is? Sense control is not denying yourself enjoyment of the senses as is usually believed to be.

You work hard to achieve success without paying attention to sense control. This makes you vulnerable to sense allurement. Then even one moment of indiscretion washes away all your good work. Lack of control has led to the downfall of some of the world's greatest leaders, sportspersons and captains of industry.

In *Vivekacūḍāmaṇi* Ādi Śaṅkarācārya describes five different species that are destroyed by a weakness for one sense object. Then he observes that a human being has an appetite for all five. How does he safeguard himself?

The examples he gives are:

(1) A moth is attracted by sight. It goes around the dancing flame till it gets scorched to death.
(2) A deer is lured by sound. Attracted by the drumbeats it comes out into the open and gets shot.
(3) A fish has a weakness for taste. It bites the bait and gets killed.
(4) A bee is attracted by smell. It enters the flower which closes in and destroys it.
(5) An elephant falls for touch. During the mating season, the elephant gets restless and falls in the trap.

Even a person who has his intellect in place, who is continually working at strengthening it, even such a person's mind is carried away forcefully by the senses. The same thought is conveyed in the Manu Smṛti. It says '*balavān indriyagrāmo vidvaṁsamapi karṣati*' — 'the group of senses is so powerful, it carries away even a wise person.'

The Purāṇas have various stories about how great sages fell prey to temptation when they were not alert. Bharata, the king-sage who had renounced his kingdom and the trappings of wealth to seek Realisation, allowed his obsession for a deer to come in the way of his goal. Legend goes that Viśvāmitra, one of the seven all-time greats among sages, was in deep meditation. Menakā, the celestial damsel, came down to dance before him and Viśvāmitra succumbed to her charms. If the likes of Bharata and Viśvāmitra could fall from their exalted positions what chance do you have? Yet you indulge in the world without any regard to strengthening the intellect, without reinforcing yourself against the assault of these enticements.

Sense objects and sense organs are inherently attracted to each other. The objects themselves are alluring. So the world tugs at you from outside. In addition there is a thrust from within towards the objects. Your sense organs are drawn towards them.

Slick advertising has made the task of withstanding this dual force even more difficult. You attempt to control your diet, but as you step out you see billboards advertising delicious food items. Pizza outlets say 'Buy one get one free'! And you yield. You go to a shop to buy one thing but the display is so attractive that you buy a lot more than you had planned. To make matters worse the credit card system fuels it with the slogan 'Buy now, pay later'!

There is a war going on between you and the world. The first line of defence on your side is the senses. The senses are first vanquished by the enemy. Next in line is the mind. In this verse He says, 'The stormy senses drag the mind to the other side'.

In verses 61 to 67 He takes a conscious detour from the line of thinking to underscore the pivotal role of the intellect. Then in verse 67 He says, 'that mind which was carried away by the senses drags the intellect away'. When your intellect goes you are destroyed. The intellect is the last bastion to fall. Thus you are in a precarious situation.

Yet, there is an optimistic note in this verse. The human being is the only species with an intellect with which he can control the senses. So the message here is — fortify your intellect, reinforce it. If the intellect slips even momentarily, you are in grave danger of being swept away by the senses. As long as the intellect is in place you are safe. Unfortunately in this day and age we concentrate on everything except the fortification of the intellect.

Verse 61

तानि सर्वाणि संयम्य युक्त आसीत मत्परः ।
वशे हि यस्येन्द्रियाणि तस्य प्रज्ञा प्रतिष्ठिता ॥ ६१ ॥

Tāni sarvāṇi saṁyamya yukta āsīta matparaḥ
Vaśe hi yasyendriyāṇi tasya prajñā pratiṣṭhitā

Restraining them all, one should sit absorbed in Me, the Highest. One whose senses are under control is indeed steadfast in Wisdom.

Here is a reference to meditation. Kṛṣṇa always prefixes his statements on meditation with 'first control the senses'. And yet most of us, with scant respect for the caution that the Bhagavad Gita advocates, start meditating without exercising sense control. He says – meditate only after having controlled all the senses. If you do not restrain the senses you cannot meditate. The mind is the instrument with which you meditate. So it has to be available to you. Today it is running all over the place because your senses are attracted by the sense objects. Kṛṣṇa does not tell us how to control the senses in this verse. He only emphasises the necessity for sense control.

Fearing victimisation, people on the spiritual path keep away from sense objects. This is hardly the solution. This is cowardice. Kṛṣṇa says it is unseemly to behave thus. A person who contacts sense objects and yet retains mastery over them is a person of self-control.

Saṁyamya means discipline, control. Sense enjoyment is not forbidden. It is an inherent aspect of human life. But if you allow it to carry on unsupervised, you will get destroyed. The famous picture of the horse chariot from the Kaṭhopaniṣad conveys this idea. The five horses represent the senses. The reins are the mind. The charioteer is the intellect. When the charioteer is alert and skilful, the reins guide the horses in the direction determined by the charioteer. Thus he reaches his destination. If the charioteer lacks the requisite skills and is not on guard, the reins are loose, the horses go whichever way they please and the chariot crashes.

Similarly when the intellect is sharp and suitably fortified, the mind and senses are guided properly towards your goal. When the intellect is undeveloped and is not vigilant, the mind fails to rein in the senses which fall for their respective sense organs. Thus you fail materially as well as spiritually.

'A Realised Person is one whose senses are under control'. This is the first step towards spiritual development.

'Having achieved this sit absorbed in Me, *Ātman*'. This is a passing reference to meditation. A controlled person's mind is, by nature, calm and contemplative. It is in meditative mode. Only then can you meditate. In meditation the intellect directs the mind to one thought without allowing it to meander into any other thought. When a seeker meditates thus, even the last thought is removed, leading to Realisation.

The next two verses 62 and 63 together tell us what happens when we do not control the senses.

Verses 62 and 63

ध्यायतो विषयान्पुंसः सङ्गस्तेषूपजायते ।
सङ्गात्संजायते कामः कामात्क्राधोऽभिजायते ॥ ६२ ॥
क्रोधाद्भवति सम्मोहः सम्मोहात्स्मृतिविभ्रमः ।
स्मृतिभ्रंशाद्बुद्धिनाशो बुद्धिनाशात्प्रणश्यति ॥ ६३ ॥

Dhyāyato viṣayānpuṁsaḥ saṅgasteṣūpajāyate
Saṅgātsañjāyate kāmaḥ kāmātkrodho'bhijāyate
Krodhādbhavati sammohaḥ sammohātsmṛtivibhramaḥ
Smṛtibhraṁśād buddhināśo buddhināśātpraṇaśyati

Pondering over objects, one gets attached to them. Attachment breeds desire, from desire anger is born. Anger leads to delusion, from delusion memory gets clouded, from clouding of memory the intellect gets destroyed, when the intellect goes one is ruined.

When the intellect is not deployed you go down the stairway to destruction. One thing leads to another and before you know it ruin stares you in the face. Only the intellect safeguards you from this predicament.

It begins with a casual thought and if you allow the thought to continue it gathers momentum. You hear of a new car.

You invest in the thought till you want to test-drive it. This is called attachment.

Then you want to buy the car. The attachment further takes shape as desire. So first you are drawn by it, then you desire it.

Anger is an aberration of desire. When an extraneous element comes in the way of your desire being fulfilled, you get angry at the disruptive element. If the loan for the car is not approved you get angry with the agent who has denied it.

When you are angry you get deluded. A teenager gets angry with his father and says things he should not say. The father also gets angry, leading to a chaotic situation. Psychologists refer to anger as 'temporary madness'. If even one member keeps his head on his shoulders such a condition is averted.

Delusion leads to the clouding of memory. In the heat of the moment son and father forget their relationship; son forgets to show respect, father forgets to show understanding.

When memory gets clouded your intellect bites the dust. The emotion builds up to such an extent that you lose the capacity to think. This destroys you. Thus step by step one thought snowballs into self-annihilation.

Stairway to destruction

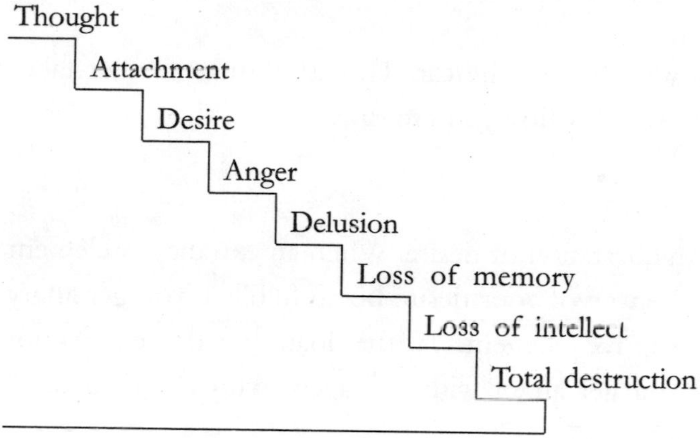

It is not physical prowess that has made the human being the ruler of the universe but the capacity of the intellect to think. This is what has put him in a commanding position. Otherwise, physically, he is no match for the animal kingdom. The intellect must be closely guarded, protected, developed. We must understand how vulnerable we are to destruction. And it all starts with one thought. Before we know it we have gone through the whole process onto total destruction. We must think through to the consequences of our actions.

Suppose your friends plan a holiday to an exotic location. They invite you to join them. You are tempted. But the intellect should immediately come into play and consider the constraints. You may not be able to afford the trip. You may also have stiff deadlines to meet. You should press the 'delete button' on the thought because it is not possible for you to act on it at this point in time.

However, if a thought is practical or is in your interest to pursue, by all means encourage it. If you feel you should study the Bhagavad Gītā, do not dismiss the thought! But examine every thought at the very first stage.

When one pathogenic, disease-causing bacterium enters your system you do not notice it. You feel fine. Having firmly ensconced itself in your body it starts multiplying. Initially you show no signs of discomfort. But the bacteria multiply at such a rate that one fine day you are hit. Then you are laid up for a number of days even if it is a minor infection. What is a bacterium? What is its power? What sophistication does a bacterium have compared to a human being? Yet that microscopic being can debilitate you.

Similarly, you entertain thoughts at random, not knowing their power. You feel, 'what can that one thought do?' But the thought takes root in your system and can destroy you. Therefore, what you need in spirituality is a 'Thought Scanner'. You need to scan every thought that enters your mind. If you do that you will be fine. If not, it will be very difficult to control the force of your thought flow. Imagine a car on a steep incline. When it starts rolling down gently, it is possible to apply the brakes and stop it. But as the car gains momentum, the brakes become more and more ineffective in halting the vehicle and it eventually crashes.

Thoughts come into your mind at such a terrific pace that most of the time you are not even aware of the kind of thoughts you are entertaining. And what is even more

dangerous is that you are entertaining negative thoughts. As an American activist said to his son, "A person may have done many injustices to you, but never ever entertain hatred towards him. The bitterness may or may not do him any harm, but it will surely destroy you." Thinking negatively can only lead to negative results for you. The other person may be blissfully unaware of what is happening in your mind. Therefore you must be extra alert to make sure that you harbour the right kind of thoughts. When you entertain thoughts which are detrimental to your well-being, you should be able to arrest them. These two verses highlight the importance of the intellect in controlling such thought patterns.

Verse 64

रागद्वेषवियुक्तैस्तु विषयानिन्द्रियैश्चरन् ।
आत्मवश्यैर्विधेयात्मा प्रसादमधिगच्छति ॥ ६४ ॥

Rāgadveṣaviyuktaistu viṣayānindriyaiścaran
Ātmavaśyairvidheyātmā prasādamadhigacchati

But the self-restrained one who has gained self-mastery becomes serene. Free from attraction and aversion, such a one moves amidst sense objects.

Here Kṛṣṇa gives the technique of sense control. Why is He asking you to control the senses? Because when you function without control, you accumulate desires. This takes you further away from the goal of Realisation and ironically desires interfere even with material success. Intemperate indulgence in the senses detracts from the goal.

The technique of sense control has two distinct parts as implied by the two words — *ātmavaśyaiḥ* (one who is self-controlled) and *vidheyātmā* (one who has achieved self-mastery). *Vidheyātmā* is also a name of Lord Viṣṇu. And Kṛṣṇa is an incarnation of Viṣṇu.

Part I

The intellect screens the thoughts in the mind so that no interaction with the senses goes ungoverned. This, in turn, is achieved in two ways.

1. Every one of us has inherent desires, attraction and repulsion towards objects. You are born with some and during your lifetime you cultivate many more. When the intellect gets marginalised and the mind takes over your activity you lose control. To become a controlled person, you should ensure that the attractions and aversions do not directly fuel action. Attractions and aversions should be scanned by the intellect and acted upon only if the intellect authorises it. This does not mean that you should deny yourself everything you like and opt for all the things you dislike. That would be frustrating. In fact the intellect may allow many of your likes. There would be only a few things that the intellect would disallow because they are detrimental to you. In such cases, abide by the intellect.

2. Fresh contact with a sense object should not create a new wave of desire in your system. The Praṣnopaniṣad explains the phenomenon of sense perception. Your mind makes contact with the world of sense objects through the five sense organs. Only then do you enjoy the experience. If the mind does not support the perception it will not register it. In other words you do not enjoy it. A busy, stressed-out executive goes home and finds a delectable meal spread before

him. But since his mind is on problems at work he eats the meal without enjoying it.

The Gītā does not debar enjoyment. It only cautions against stirring up 'action replays' in the mind after the experience is over. Do not let the mind loiter in bygone enjoyments. If you tarry there, you create a new wave of desire. Moreover, when the body moves to the next experience you are not able to enjoy the new contact. The mind is still savouring the thought of the previous experience. Let the enjoyment go on but do not persist in its thought. **Linger and you will languish**.

All the while the mind is engaged in past revelry and at no point of time are you enjoying the present experience. So the Bhagavad Gītā, in advocating sense control, is giving back the enjoyment you have lost.

Evoking past enjoyments is like chewing the cud. When cattle return to their sheds after grazing all day, they regurgitate their food and chew it again. In the same manner, you enjoy many experiences during the day. Later, you revive those enjoyments in your mind. Kṛṣṇa recommends a formula by which you enjoy each moment to the fullest without adding to your burden of desires.

So in Part I the intellect is used to prevent:

1. Existing attractions and aversions from directly fuelling actions.

2. Fresh experiences from sparking off a new trajectory of craving.

Part II

As long as you value sense enjoyment you can never really control the senses. What is required then is growth to a higher dimension. A lofty goal makes it easier for the intellect to control the senses.

The person who has just embarked on the spiritual journey still has desires for sense enjoyment. He is vulnerable to the lure of the senses. But he has also been introduced to higher values and understands there are far more significant things in life to aspire for. He is determined not to allow his weakness for the senses to come in the way of his achieving the higher. So he restricts sense contact to enable him to pursue his goal. Corporate executives may refrain from drinking during the week to focus on work but give vent to their penchant for alcohol over the weekend. Sportspersons are careful about their diet while preparing for a big event. But they allow themselves a treat when the event is over. Spiritual aspirants restrict sense enjoyment to the extent necessary but incorporate moments of enjoyment in their discipline.

In this intermediate phase a certain degree of physical abstinence is required until you establish yourself at the higher level.

Once you are secure in the higher the temptation itself ceases.

The lower no longer attracts the mind. Just as an adult is no longer tempted by toys. However when the occasion arises he can engage in a game of scrabble with his child or play 'hearts' on his laptop while waiting to board a flight. He is in full control because his mind is not hankering after the game. It is absorbed in higher aspirations.

At this stage sense control comes as a result of wisdom. The corporate executive who earlier had a weakness for alcohol finds fulfillment in more exciting things. The sportsperson values health so much that the taste for unhealthy indulgence vanishes. The spiritual aspirant has transcended his physical desires and is enjoying far more satisfying pursuits. He is convinced that everything in the world is fragile and precarious. He has access to that which is permanent, unchanging. Now any amount of sense contact fails to shake him from his exalted state.

This concept has been illustrated in the personalities of Kṛṣṇa and Durvāsa. Kṛṣṇa was called a *nitya brahmacāri,* meaning eternal celibate. Yet he had 16,000 wives! Durvāsa was called *nitya upavāsi*, one who always fasts. But he consumed large quantities of food.

Hence control has no reference to the amount of contact with the sense object. Control only means intellectual governance. Never should you allow even one thought to go the sense object without the specific approval of the 'llect.

'y is in its infancy when it revels in *bhoga*, sense

enjoyment. You achieve sense control when there is a paradigm shift from *bhoga* to *yoga* — higher levels of enjoyment culminating in *Ātman*. If you do not rise from *bhoga* to *yoga*, you will be afflicted by *roga* — disease at body level and dis-ease at mind level. Moreover you will not be able to effectively control the senses.

Yoga is achieved when you escalate from *viṣayānanda* (sense enjoyment) through *bhajanānanda* (emotional and intellectual delights) to *Brahmānanda* (spiritual ecstasy). As you rise to the emotional and intellectual planes, sense enjoyment loses its charm. The senses no longer have a hold on you. Thus control becomes easy. Finally, when you access the infinite joy of the Spirit even emotional and intellectual delights become meaningless. Nothing in the world tempts you. The mind becomes free to focus on the goal of Realisation.

Thus in summary, the two methods to control are:

Part I: Use your intellect to supervise and guide sense contact.

Part II: Escalate to higher realms of enjoyment as a result of which the lower no longer tempts you.

The result of leading a life of self-control is peace. That elusive sense of serenity. This is depicted by the sweet (*prasāda*) distributed after a *pūjā* or spiritual worship. Peop[illegible] have not been educated on subtler levels of gratifica[illegible] Sense enjoyment is all they know. Thus the sens[illegible] powerful and the intellect is weak. The sensory syst[illegible]

sway over the intellect. As a result you fall for every passing fancy. And the battle with the senses is lost. Hence, the whole world is in a state of disquiet and disturbance. Internal strife manifests as external conflict between people, communities and nations. Peace is the need of the hour and it can come only through self-control. Thus, development of the intellect is of paramount importance.

Verse 65

प्रसादे सर्वदुःखानां हानिरस्योपजायते ।
प्रसन्नचेतसो ह्याशु बुद्धिः पर्यवतिष्ठते ॥ ६५ ॥

Prasāde sarvaduḥkhānāṁ hānirasyopajāyate
Prasannacetaso hyāśu buddhiḥ paryavatiṣṭhate

All sorrows end in (that) serenity. The serene one's intellect is soon steadied.

In verse 64, He gave us the formula for self-control. Once the intellect governs the impulses of the mind by default, all your actions become benign. When attractions and aversions drive activities the actions turn malignant. And your mind should not regurgitate and dwell on the enjoyment after the contact with the object ceases. Lastly, when you grow to access higher planes of happiness the senses lose their charm. They no longer interfere with the pursuit of the Divine. And Kṛṣṇa says 'One who has controlled the senses achieves peace'.

In this verse He says, "All your sorrows are destroyed in that peace which you have obtained as a result of practising self-control". In a peaceful, tranquil mind the intellect becomes sharp. Even sportspersons accept that they achieve peak

performance only when their mind is relaxed. Athletes acknowledge that among the finalists, the difference between them is minimal. The mind determines whether you win or lose. You gain clarity of thinking only with a relaxed mind. You become efficient, successful and prosperous.

When you control the senses you become successful as well as happy. These two attributes are almost always mutually exclusive. A person who achieves success seems to lose happiness. And success eludes a happy person. But you want a combination of both. You achieve that amalgam through the Gītā. So the endeavour should be to have a peaceful mind and a focussed intellect. If you have these two you achieve both material and spiritual excellence. External enrichment is possible only when the mind is enriched.

Verse 66

नास्ति बुद्धिरयुक्तस्य न चायुक्तस्य भावना।
न चाभावयतः शान्तिरशान्तस्य कुतः सुखम् ॥ ६६ ॥

Nāsti buddhirayuktasya na cāyuktasya bhāvanā
Na cābhāvayataḥ śāntiraśāntasya kutaḥ sukham

The *ayukta* (disunited) has neither intellect nor *bhāvanā* (contemplation) and without *bhāvanā* there can be no peace; how will there be happiness for the one without peace?

The verse starts by saying that there is no intellect for the *ayukta* — one who is not yoked to a higher ideal, the highest being *Ātman*. The higher the goal to which one is aligned, the greater the serenity. And stronger the intellect. When you have fixed a goal the intellect guides your actions towards it. And weeds out anything that thwarts the pursuit of your goal. This discipline calms the mind and makes it contemplative. Only a calm mind can perceive the play of Divinity in the world. When you are disturbed you are unable to see the splendour of nature. *Bhāvanā* means opening your mind to the Divine.

You are in a prison of your own making. In a priso

convict has no freedom to choose when to eat, what to eat, what to wear or what to do. Everything is decided by the prison authorities. Similarly, in life you are forced to dance to the tune of the body, mind and intellect. Your entire life is consumed in catering to their demands. You have no choice to act independently. A wise prisoner conducts himself such that he gets released as soon as possible, preferably on parole. He has no interest in the prison activities. His real life is out there in the world.

When you become aware of your plight in the prison of life you lose interest in the happenings of the world. You understand your real life lies beyond it all. This is only your 'reel' life. Liberation becomes your goal. Every activity is then dedicated to obtaining release from the self-imposed sentence. And the Gītā promises instant parole, here and now! Your intellect is focussed on freedom. And your mind is devoted to that goal.

The combination of intellectual focus and devotion brings about saturation of thought. This culminates in crystallisation — Realisation. Just as crystals form when a solution of copper sulphate is saturated. When the mind and intellect are converged on the goal of Realisation, there is a sudden leap of consciousness and the solution to the mystery of life unfolds before you.

Without this process of saturation and crystallisation there can be no peace. And one who is not at peace cannot be happy.

If we go back to verse 60, He says, 'the senses carry away the mind'. In verse 61 He says, 'restrain the senses first'. In verses 62 and 63 He gives the stairway to destruction. When the intellect is not alert, one thought is enough to destroy you. Just as when your immune system is not strong, one bacterium is enough to cause infection. In verse 64, He gives the prescription for sense control and if you follow it, you get peace. In verse 65, He says 'that peace leads to a sharp intellect'. Here, He says 'without control, there is neither peace nor happiness'. He deviates in verses 61 to 66 to explain the importance of the intellect. In 67, He connects with verse 60 and says 'that mind which has been dragged by the senses waylays the intellect'.

Verse 67

इन्द्रियाणां हि चरतां यन्मनोऽनुविधीयते ।
तदस्य हरति प्रज्ञां वायुर्नावमिवाम्भसि ।। ६७ ।।

Indriyāṇāṁ hi caratāṁ yanmano'nuvidhīyate
Tadasya harati prajñāṁ vayurnāvamivāmbhasi

Following the restive senses, the mind pulls one's discrimination away as the wind pulls away a boat in water.

Here He uses a famous metaphor used in the scriptures to represent a human being's journey from the shore of mortality to that of Immortality.

The comparisons are as follows:
Boat – the individual journeying through life.
Ocean – the world, with its ups and downs. Just as the ocean is characterised by waves.
Wind – stormy cravings of the mind.
Captain – the intellect, '*buddhi*'. The intellect steers you through the challenges of life. Like the captain who guides the boat through the choppy sea.
Compass – the conscience, subtle intellect. The compass always points north. Similarly the conscience always points

towards the higher, *Ātman*. Be it a sage or a criminal, every one has a conscience. When you are inundated with desires the voice of conscience gets drowned.

Harbour – if you follow the conscience you reach the harbour, the peace that comes when you dedicatedly follow your course.

Other shore – the shore of Immortality.

The metaphor fits perfectly. When there is a gale, the ocean is turbulent and the boat capsizes. The same thing happens to you when you unintelligently allow the passions of your mind to take over your personality. You entertain a thought here, fall for a desire there, and it seems harmless. If you continue in the same manner it overturns your personality. But a strong intellect guided by the conscience steers you through the challenges of life and you reach the harbour of peace. With a peaceful mind you meditate. Meditation removes the last traces of thought and you reach the shore of Realisation. This is the purpose of our existence. All of us are born in the world only to reach this destination.

So the choice is yours. Do you want to be tossed and turned by the waves of life and get shipwrecked, like so many others? Or do you want to follow the intellect, ride smoothly through life and get to the other shore? You can pursue your profession, you can have a family, you can enjoy life but in and through all this there must be this focus. Why am I born in this world? What is my mission, my *raison d'être*? It is not just to live a mechanical life. What are you a human being for? As the scriptures say, the sole purpose of human

existence is to reach God. When you embark upon this journey, there will be challenges and hindrances. You must overcome them and pursue the goal with sincerity and dedication. Give your mind a higher mission, a nobler goal.

When you are inspired with the higher, the mind automatically refrains from sense indulgence. It is not possible to control the senses by merely denying yourself. It is necessary to substitute the baser desires with a higher one.

Verse 68

तस्माद्यस्य महाबाहो निगृहीतानि सर्वशः ।
इन्द्रियाणीन्द्रियार्थेभ्यस्तस्य प्रज्ञा प्रतिष्ठिता ॥ ६८ ॥

Tasmādyasya Mahābāho nigṛhītāni sarvaśaḥ
Indriyāṇīndriyārthebhyastasya prajñā pratiṣṭhitā

Therefore, one is established in Wisdom when one's senses are wholly withdrawn from sense objects, O Mahābāho (mighty-armed one).

He calls Arjuna *'Mahābāho'*, meaning 'mighty armed one' because he was a warrior renowned for his exceptional courage and bravery. He had emerged victorious in many battles. He was a man of the world with the skill and expertise to conquer it. Kṛṣṇa suggests, "External victories are meaningless unless you conquer the inner kingdom". Arjuna, who was well qualified to tackle external challenges, failed in the conquest of his inner self.

Like Arjuna, you are competent enough to conquer the challenges that are outside of you. But you lack the knowledge and expertise to conquer your inner self. Unless you do this, you cannot succeed in life. If you do not fortify yourself with this knowledge, sooner or later you will be in

Arjuna's condition – crestfallen, unable to face adversity. Therefore Kṛṣṇa recommends that you put in a little effort at strengthening your inner personality alongside external triumphs.

A perfect Person is one whose senses are wholly withdrawn from sense objects. All the senses have to be controlled. Most people are vulnerable to one or two senses. It is these weak spots that need to be plugged. A person who has a weakness for food may be surprisingly disciplined in other areas. Another may have a controlled diet but succumb to the lure of TV. Perfection means control of all senses. One weakness is enough to drain all your inner resources. Therefore you should have an overall perspective and safeguard yourself in all areas.

No other species needs to exercise control. They have an in-built discipline that governs their actions. It is the human being alone who needs to control himself. Because he has freedom of choice. In today's world people have a great deal of freedom but the requisite discipline and intellectual strength is lacking. They are beset with all kinds of problems and cannot enjoy that freedom.

Science and technology have taken great strides in improving the world. Yet in this world which offers enhanced enjoyment, the human being's happiness has dwindled. In spite of the vastly better world around him, he is unable to enjoy it. The Bhagavad Gītā restores that enjoyment, offers permanent happiness.

Verse 69

या निशा सर्वभूतानां तस्यां जागर्ति संयमी ।
यस्यां जाग्रति भूतानि सा निशा पश्यतो मुनेः ॥ ६९ ॥

Yā niśā sarvabhūtānāṁ tasyāṁ jagarti saṁyamī
Yasyāṁ jagrati bhūtāni sā niśā paśyato muneḥ

The self-controlled one awakes in that which is night to all beings. That in which all beings are awake is night to the seer, the *muni* (sage).

In this verse, Kṛṣṇa makes an interesting observation. The world being the same, the realised Person's experience is totally different from that of the common man. You experience finitude and get crushed by the wheels of change. Everything in the world perishes. In the same world, a realised Person sees Infinity. He sees the changeless foundation behind all the changes that are taking place. His focus is on the Imperishable. These are two completely opposite experiences, like day and night. Night signifies ignorance. You are unaware of Infinity but very much tuned in to the finite things of the world. You experience limitation because of your identification with the body, mind and intellect which are limited.

The mighty sun above has many reflections. Reflected suns

appear wherever reflecting surfaces are present. The mirrored sun assumes the properties of the reflecting surface and loses its original qualities. When the sun is reflected in a drop of rain it becomes minuscule. When reflected in a frozen lake, it is cold. Similarly, you are that infinite, all pervading force '*Ātman*'. A reflected self appears wherever there is a body, mind and intellect. That reflected self loses its Infinity and takes on the properties of the body, mind and intellect. This is what causes all the problems. You see limitations, you see finitude, because your attention is on the reflected self. A realised Person sees a completely different picture. He sees the original *Ātman* divested of the distortions of the body, mind and intellect.

This concept applies even in the relative sense. The contemplative one goes to bed early and is an early riser. The sensual one is awake through the night and sleeps till late in the day. A spiritual person has a positive attitude in life; a sensualist is negative and agitated. An inward-looking person is an optimist, seeing the brighter side of life. A worldly person is a pessimist, seeing only the negatives in life. A spiritual person is invariably a giver, a materialist is a taker.

Verse 70

आपूर्यमाणमचलप्रतिष्ठं समुद्रमापः प्रविशन्ति यद्वत् ।
तद्वत्कामा यं प्रविशन्ति सर्वे स शान्तिमाप्नोति न कामकामी ॥ ७० ॥

Āpūryamāṇamacalapratiṣṭhaṁ samudramāpaḥ praviśanti yadvat
Tadvatkāmā yaṁ praviśanti sarve sa śāntimāpnoti na kāmakāmī

As the ocean which, filled from all sides with waters entering it, remains still, so one in whom all objects of desire enter obtains peace, not the desirer of desires.

This verse is extracted from the Muṇḍaka Upaniṣad. The Upaniṣad says, 'As rivers flowing disappear in the ocean losing name and form, the wise one free from name and form attains the effulgent *Puruṣa*'. It gives the example of rivers entering the ocean. Each river is distinct and different from the other. But the moment they enter the ocean they lose their individual properties and become one with the ocean.

Kṛṣṇa compares the ocean with the state of Realisation. When a person realises the Self, the objects and beings of the world enter him but they do not make any difference to him. Just as when millions of gallons of water from the rivers enter the ocean, it does not make any difference to the ocean. The salinity does not decrease; the composition of

the ocean does not change. It remains the same because the ocean is vast.

The *sthitaprajña* has reached the state of infinite Happiness. All of us are chasing happiness and yet nobody seems to know where it lies or how to get it. The Gītā gives us a formula for happiness. The formula as enunciated by Tilak in 'Gītā Rahasya' is

$$\text{Happiness} = \frac{\text{Number of desires actualised}}{\text{Number of desires harboured}}$$

If you want to increase the quotient you must either increase the numerator or decrease the denominator. Preferably both. You go all out to increase the numerator believing it will enhance your happiness. But are you achieving it? When one desire gets fulfilled, you are happy for a while but simultaneously, without your realising it, the denominator also increases. As a result your happiness actually reduces. Everywhere you find attractive shop displays. Products are being advertised aggressively, stoking the fires of desire. As a result you fulfil a few desires, and the numerator increases a bit, but the denominator increases at a faster rate. Thus your happiness is constantly diminishing.

A lady wants new curtains for her living room. She gets them, only to discover that the upholstery doesn't match with the curtains. So she re-upholsters the living room furniture. But then the walls look old in comparison. So she decides to paint the room. But now she has to paint the

whole house. Thus one thing leads to another and at the end of it all she finds her savings significantly depleted. She began by fulfilling one desire. But that one desire led to the cultivation of numerous other desires.

So if you want your happiness to increase, what you need to do is just deal with the denominator. The numerator is not really relevant. If you increase the numerator, your happiness will increase. But any increase in the denominator will negate it. Besides however much you increase the numerator you can never get infinite happiness. On the other hand if you reduce the denominator your happiness increases by leaps and bounds. And if you are able to bring it down to zero you achieve infinite Happiness. That is exactly what you are looking for. The spiritual path is designed to get you to that infinite Happiness. Once you attain Infinity, anything that is added on does not make any difference.

This is true even mathematically. Anything added to or subtracted from infinity still gives infinity.

'One in whom all objects of desire enter attains peace, not the desirer of objects'. The person who deals with the denominator achieves peace, not the person who is working on the numerator.

You may or may not fulfil your desires. But there must be some programme to deal with the denominator if you are serious about attaining happiness. Otherwise you will be stuck with a whole lot of desires and you won't know how to manage them.

Verse 71

विहाय कामान्यः सर्वान्पुमांश्चरति निःस्पृहः ।
निर्ममो निरहङ्कारः स शान्तिमधिगच्छति ।। ७१ ।।

Vihāya kāmānyaḥ sarvānpumaṁścarati niḥspṛhaḥ
Nirmamo nirahaṅkāraḥ sa śāntimadhigacchati

That person attains peace, who relinquishing all desires, lives without longing, mineness or egoism.

In verses 69 to 72 Kṛṣṇa gives a recap of His answer. Arjuna's question in verse 54 is: 'Who is a perfect Person, what is his description?' In verse 55 Kṛṣṇa defines the realised Person: 'One who has totally abandoned all desires from the mind and is fulfilled in the Self by the Self'. In verse 70 He explains the concept further. Here He asserts that only the person who has renounced desire attains peace.

The problem with us is not in the possession of external objects. The problem is with the multiplication of desires in the mind. As long as you have a desire, you become dependent. You become a slave, a beggar, to the object of desire. This is an unintelligent thing to do. So have the object, but not the desire. You can have the world at your feet, but never should you crave for or hanker after anything. And we

have already seen how to relinquish desire. Escalate to the higher desire and the lower one drops.

From infancy to adulthood this escalation is natural. But having reached adulthood you need to put in effort to move to spiritual adulthood which is the state of Realisation. In order to grow to that stage you need knowledge of the higher. Once you gain knowledge of the higher, the lower desires automatically drop.

There is a story of a neighbouring country in which there was a revolution and the royal family had to seek refuge in India. When the situation improved the king, the queen and the courtiers returned, leaving the infant prince in the safe hands of their trusted governess in Mumbai. They told her not to tell anyone that he was the prince, not even the little heir himself.

Soon thereafter the entire royal family was put to death. The prince was the only surviving member, the heir to the throne. There was anarchy in the state for several years. When peace returned, the loyal subjects wanted their king back. They sent their representatives all over Mumbai to look for the prince. The prince and his governess were living in the streets in abject poverty. The prince was a beggar. He would get alms one day and celebrate and get nothing the next day and be dejected. This was his life.

One day he encountered the royal entourage. They were speaking in a strange language which he had heard his

governess speak. So he ran and called her out. She realised that they were the courtiers in search of the prince and was ecstatic. However due to security reasons she did not divulge the truth to the prince. She only said they were friends and had invited them to their hometown.

On arrival in their capital they told the prince the whole truth. Initially he was uncomfortable in his new role and wanted to return to Mumbai. But gradually he got used to it and soon became a good king. A few years later he came to India on a state visit. One day in Mumbai, he dodged his security personnel, wore his beggar's attire and went to the same area where he used to beg until recently. Some people gave him alms, others didn't.

What is the difference between his experiences now and earlier? He is the king now. But he was king even then. Then what has contributed to his newfound freedom? Until a few years ago even though he was the king he did not know he was king. It is the ignorance of his kingship that made him a victim of circumstance. When somebody was good to him, he was thrilled. If somebody was unpleasant, he was dejected. He went through the ups and downs of life because he did not know he was king. Now he is going through the same experiences. But he is enjoying every moment of the few hours as a beggar. Because he now **knows** he is king.

So all you have to do is understand who you really are. Once you understand that you are a king, *Ātman*, you remain unaffected through the highs and lows, the achievements

and the setbacks of life. You retain the equanimity and exhilaration of kingship through all your experiences. So knowledge is the key. Knowledge of your Self. Not of the Gītā or the scriptures. In '*Ātmabodha*' Śaṅkarācārya says: 'Of all spiritual disciplines knowledge of Self is the direct means to liberation'. Once you know your true identity you live in the world in a totally different manner — detached, unaffected, blissful.

Verse 72

एषा ब्राह्मी स्थितिः पार्थ नैनां प्राप्य विमुह्यति ।
स्थित्वास्यामन्तकालेऽपि ब्रह्मनिर्वाणमृच्छति ।। ७२ ।।

Esā Brāhmī sthitiḥ Pārtha naināṁ prāpya vimuhyati
Sthitvāsyāmantakāle'pi brahmanirvāṇamṛcchati

O Pārtha, this is the nature of *Brahman*. Having attained this nobody is deluded. Remaining in it one attains *nirvāṇa* (union with *Brahman*) even after death.

In this verse He beautifully encapsulates the entire 19 verses. He endorses the concept of '*jīvan mukti*' which means you can gain the stage of Realisation even here, while living in the world. There is another concept called '*videhamukti*' which says that you have to physically die to get to the state of Realisation. Throughout the Gītā, Kṛṣṇa says you can get it 'here and now'. He does not promise a speculative, post-mortem paradise. All you have to do is want it. Then you put in efforts to get it.

You might wonder having reached some level of spiritual development what happens when you die? The Gītā says having got it, there is no return. In the material world you work to make money, but you might lose it. Or a person aspires for and attains social status but one slip and it is

gone. You tend to believe that the same thing will happen in the spiritual field. But spiritual assets once obtained never go. Your spiritual stock only appreciates. No loss, only gain. Kṛṣṇa gives us this assurance. He says 'even at the end of life one does not lose the state of *nirvāṇa* — union with *Brahman*'. It continues even after death.

This is not true of any other achievement. How futile it is to pursue material ends. With the death of the body all is lost. You cannot take your assets with you. You cannot take your home or even your family with you. You cannot access your worldly knowledge after death. The only thing you carry along is your spiritual status, the level and quality of your mind and intellect. So it would be wise to invest a little time and effort in safeguarding your future interest.

Inherent in the description of a person of Realisation is the path to get there. Thus we have a clear goal to aspire for. And a method by which to get there.

As Indians, this knowledge is our inheritance. It is our wealth. If we are able to make use of it, bring it out of the books and into our lives, we can work miracles in the world not only for ourselves but also for humanity at large. Right through history this country has been a beacon light for humanity. The unfortunate part is that we are not making use of it. So the appeal here by Kṛṣṇa is — use this knowledge, develop yourself. Become a *sthitaprajña* — a perfect Person.